THE CONTEMPORARY SHAKESPEARE

Edited by A. L. Rowse

All's Well That Ends Well

Modern Text with Introduction

UNIVERSITY PRESS OF AMERICA

Copyright © 1985 by A.L. Rowse

University Press of America,® Inc.

4720 Boston Way
Lanham, MD 20706

3 Henrietta Street
London WC2E 8LU England

Printed in the United States of America

Distributed to the trade by The Scribner Book Companies

Library of Congress Cataloging in Publication Data

Shakespeare, William, 1564-1616.
  All's well that ends well.

  (The Contemporary Shakespeare)
  I. Rowse, A. L. (Alfred Leslie), 1903-   .
II. Title. III. Series: Shakespeare, William, 1564-
1616. Plays (University Press of America : Pbk. ed.)
PR2801.A2R64   1985   822.3'3   85-678
ISBN 0-8191-3917-3 (pbk.)

This play is also available as part of Volume III in a seven volume
clothbound and slipcased set.

Book design by Leon Bolognese

WHY A CONTEMPORARY SHAKESPEARE?

The starting point of my project was when I learned both from television and in education, that Shakespeare is being increasingly dropped in schools and colleges because of the difficulty of the language. In some cases, I gather, they are given just a synopsis of the play, then the teacher or professor embroiders from his notes.

This is deplorable. We do not want Shakespeare progressively dropped because of superfluous difficulties that can be removed, skilfully, conservatively, keeping to every line of the text. Nor must we look at the question statically, for this state of affairs will worsen as time goes on and we get further away from the language of 400 years ago—difficult enough in all conscience now.

We must begin by ridding our mind of prejudice, i.e. we must not pre-judge the matter. A friend of mine on New York radio said that he was 'appalled' at the very idea; but when he heard my exposition of what was proposed he found it reasonable and convincing.

Just remember, I do not need it myself: *I live in the Elizabethan age*, Shakespeare's time, and have done for years, and am familiar with its language, and his. But even for me there are still difficulties—still more for modern people, whom I am out to help.

Who, precisely?

Not only students at school and in college, but all readers of Shakespeare. Not only those, but all viewers of the plays, in the theatre, on radio and television—actors too, who increasingly find pronunciation of the words difficult, particularly obsolete ones—and there are many, besides the difficulty of accentuation.

The difficulties are naturally far greater for non-English-speaking peoples. We must remember that he is our greatest asset, and that other peoples use him a great deal in learning our language. There are no Iron Curtains for him—though, during Mao's Cultural Revolution in China, he was prohibited. Now that the ban has been lifted, I learn that the Chinese in thousands flock to his plays.

Now, a good deal that was grammatical four hundred years ago is positively ungrammatical today. We might begin by removing what is no longer good grammar.

For example: plural subjects with a verb in the singular:

'Is Bushy, Green and the earl of Wiltshire dead?' Any objection to replacing 'is' correctly by 'are'? Certainly not. I notice that some modern editions already correct—

These high wild hills and rough uneven ways
Draws out our miles and makes them wearisome

to 'draw' and 'make', quite sensibly. Then, why not go further and regularise this Elizabethan usage to modern, consistently throughout?

Similarly with archaic double negatives—'Nor shall you not think neither'—and double comparatives: 'this is more worser than before.' There are hundreds of instances of what is now just bad grammar to begin with.

There must be a few thousand instances of superfluous subjunctives to reduce to simplicity and sense. Today we use the subjunctive occasionally after 'if', when we say 'if it be'. But we mostly say today 'if it is'. Now Shakespeare has hundreds of subjunctives, not only after if, but after though, although, unless, lest, whether, until, till, etc.

I see no point whatever in retaining them. They only add superfluous trouble in learning English, when the great appeal of our language as a world-language is precisely that it has less grammar to learn than almost any. Russian is unbelievably complicated. Inflected languages—German is like Latin in this respect—are really rather backward; it has been a great recommendation that English has been more progressive in this respect in simplifying itself.

Now we can go further along this line: keep a few subjunctives, if you must, but reduce them to a minimum.

Let us come to the verb. It is a great recommendation to modern English that our verbs are comparatively simple to conjugate — unlike even French, for example. In the Elizabethan age there was a great deal more of it, and some of it inconsistent in modern usage. Take Shakespeare's,

'Where is thy husband now? Where be thy brothers?'

Nothing is lost by rendering this as we should today:

Where is your husband now? Where are your brothers?

And so on.

The second and third person singular—all those shouldsts and wouldsts, wilts and shalts, haths and doths, have become completely obsolete. Here a vast simplification may be effected—with no loss as far as I can see, and with advantages from several points of view.

For example, 'st' at the end of a word is rather difficult to say, and more difficult even for us when it is succeeded by a word beginning with 'th'. Try saying, 'Why usurpedst thou this?' Foreigners have the greatest difficulty in pronouncing our 'th' anyway—many never succeed in getting it round their tongues. Many of these tongue-twisters even for us proliferate in Shakespeare, and I see no objection to getting rid of *superfluous* difficulties. Much easier for people to say, 'Why did you usurp this?'—the same number of syllables too.

This pre-supposes getting rid of almost all thous and thees and thines. I have no objection to keeping a few here and there, if needed for a rhyme—even then they are sometimes not necessary.

Some words in Shakespeare have changed their meaning into the exact opposite: we ought to remove that stumbling-block. When Hamlet says, 'By heaven, I'll make a ghost of him that *lets* me', he means *stops*; and we should replace it by stops, or holds me. Shakespeare regularly uses the word 'owe' where we should say own: the meaning has changed. Take a line like, 'Thou dost here usurp the name thou ow'st not': we should say, 'You do here usurp the name you own not', with the bonus of getting rid of two ugly 'sts'.

The word 'presently' in the Elizabethan age did not mean in a few minutes or so, but immediately—instantly has the same number of syllables. 'Prevent' then had its Latin meaning, to go before, or forestall. Shakespeare frequently uses the word 'still' for always or ever.

Let us take the case of many archaic forms of words, simple one-syllable words that can be replaced without the slightest difference to the scansion: 'sith' for since, 'wrack' for wreck, 'holp' for helped, 'writ' for wrote, 'brake' for broke, 'spake' for spoke, 'bare' for bore, etc.

These give no trouble, nor do a lot of other words that he uses: 'repeal' for recall, 'reproof' for disproof, 'decline' for incline. A few words do give more trouble. The linguistic scholar, C. T. Onions, notes that it is sometimes difficult to give the precise meaning Shakespeare attaches to the word 'conceit'; it usually means thought, or fancy, or concept. I do not know that it ever has our meaning; actually the word 'conceited' with him means ingenious or fantastic, as 'artificial' with Elizabethans meant artistic or ingenious.

There is a whole class of words that have completely gone out, of which moderns do not know the meaning. I find no harm in replacing the word 'coistrel' by rascal, which is what it means—actually it has much the same sound—or 'coil' by fuss; we find 'accite' for summon, 'indigest' for formless. Hamlet's word 'reechy', for the incestuous kisses of his mother and her brother-in-law, has gone out of use: the nearest word, I suppose, would be reeky, but filthy would be a suitable modern equivalent.

In many cases it is extraordinary how little one would need to change, how conservative one could be. Take Hamlet's famous soliloquy, 'To be or not to be.' I find only two words that moderns would not know the meaning of, and one of those we might guess:

> . . .When he himself might his *quietus* make
> With a bare bodkin? Who would *fardels* bear. . .

'Quietus' means put paid; Elizabethans wrote the Latin 'quietus est' at the bottom of a bill that was paid—when it was—to say that it was settled. So that you could replace 'quietus' by settlement, same number of syllables, though not the same accentuation; so I would prefer to use the word acquittance, which has both.

'Fardels' means burdens; I see no objection to rendering, 'Who would burdens bear'—same meaning, same number of syllables, same accent: quite simple. I expect all the ladies to know what a bodkin is: a long pin, or skewer.

Now let us take something really difficult—perhaps the most difficult passage to render in all Shakespeare. It is the virtuoso comic piece describing all the diseases that horseflesh is heir to, in *The Taming of the Shrew*. The horse is Petruchio's. President Reagan tells me that this is the one Shakespearean part that he played—and a very gallant one too. In Britain last year we saw a fine performance of his on horseback in Windsor Park alongside of Queen Elizabeth II—very familiar ground to William Shakespeare and Queen Elizabeth I, as we know from *The Merry Wives of Windsor*.

Here is a headache for us: Petruchio's horse (not President Reagan's steed) was 'possessed with the glanders, and like to mose in the chine; troubled with the lampass, infected with the fashions, full of windgalls, sped with spavins, rayed with the yellows, past cure of the fives, stark spoiled with the staggers, begnawn with the bots; swayed in the back, and shoulder-shotten; near-legged before, and with a half-cheeked bit, and a headstall of sheep's leather', etc.

What on earth are we to make of that? No doubt it raised a laugh with Elizabethans, much more familiarly acquainted with horseflesh than we are; but I doubt if Hollywood was able to produce a nag for Reagan that qualified in all these respects.

Now, even without his horsemanship, we can clear one fence at the outset: 'mose in the chine'. Pages of superfluous commentary have been devoted to that word 'mose'. There was no such Elizabethan word: it was simply a printer's misprint for 'mourn', meaning dripping or running; so it suggests a running sore. You would need to consult the *Oxford English Dictionary*, compiled on historical lines, for some of the words, others like 'glanders' country folk know and we can guess.

So I would suggest a rendering something like this: 'possessed with glanders, and with a running sore in the back; troubled in the gums, and infected in the glands; full of galls in the fetlocks and swollen in the joints; yellow with jaundice, past cure of the strangles; stark spoiled with the staggers, and gnawed by worms; swayed in the back and shoulder put out; near-legged before, and with a half-cheeked bit and headgear of sheep's leather', etc. That at least makes it intelligible.

Oddly enough, one encounters the greatest difficulty with the least important words and phrases, Elizabethan expletives and malapropisms, or salutations like God 'ild you, Godden, for God shield you, Good-even, and so on. 'God's wounds' was Elizabeth I's favourite swearword; it appears frequently enough in Victorian novels as 'Zounds'— I have never heard anyone use it. The word 'Marry!', as in the phrase 'Marry come up!' has similarly gone out, though a very old gentleman at All Souls, Sir Charles Oman, had heard the phrase in the back-streets of Oxford just after the 1914-18 war. 'Whoreson' is frequent on the lips of coarse fellows in Shakespeare: the equivalent in Britain today would be bloody, in America (I suppose) s.o.b.

Relative pronouns, who and which: today we use who for persons, which for things. In Elizabethan times the two were hardly distinguished and were interchangeable. Provokingly Shakespeare used the personal relative 'who' more frequently for impersonal objects, rivers, buildings, towns; and then he no less frequently uses 'which' for persons. This calls out to be regularised for the modern reader.

Other usages are more confusing. The word 'cousin'

was used far more widely by the Elizabethans for their kin: it included nephews, for instance. Thus it is confusing in the English History plays to find a whole lot of nephews—like Richard III's, whom he had made away with in the Tower of London—referred to and addressed as cousins. That needs regularisation today, in the interests of historical accuracy and to get the relationship clear. The word 'niece' was sometimes used of a grandchild—in fact this is the word Shakespeare used in his will for his little grand-daughter Elizabeth, his eventual heiress who ended up as Lady Barnard, leaving money to her poor relations the Hathaways at Stratford. The Latin word *neptis*, from which niece comes also meant grandchild—Shakespeare's grammar-school education at Stratford was in Latin, and this shows you that he often thought of a word in terms of its Latin derivation.

Malapropisms, misuse of words, sometimes mistaking of meanings, are frequent with uneducated people, and sometimes not only with those. Shakespeare transcribed them from lower-class life to raise a laugh, more frequently than any writer for the purpose. They are an endearing feature of the talk of Mistress Quickly, hostess of the Boar's Inn in East Cheapside, and we have no difficulty in making out what she means. But in case some of us do, and for the benefit of non-native English speakers, I propose the correct word in brackets afterwards: 'You have brought her into such a canaries [quandary]. . .and she's as fartuous [virtuous] a civil, modest wife. . .'

Abbreviations: Shakespeare's text is starred—and in my view, marred—by innumerable abbreviations, which not only look ugly on the page but are sometimes difficult to pronounce. It is not easy to pronounce 'is't', or 'in't', or 'on't', and some others: if we cannot get rid of them altogether they should be drastically reduced. Similarly with 'i'th'', 'o'th'', with which the later plays are liberally bespattered, for "in the" or "of the."

We also have a quite unnecessary spattering of apostrophes in practically all editions of the plays—''d' for the past participle, e.g. 'gather'd'. Surely it is much better to regularise the past participle 'ed', e.g. gathered; and when the last syllable is, far less frequently, to be pronounced, then accent it, gatherèd.

This leads into the technical question of scansion, where a practising poet is necessary to get the accents right, to help the reader, and still more the actor. Most people will hardly notice that, very often, the frequent ending of words in 'ion', like reputation, has to be pronounced with two syllables at the end. So I propose to accent this when necessary, e.g. reputatiòn. I have noticed the word 'ocean' as tri-syllabic, so I accent it, to help, oceàn. A number of words which to us are monosyllables were pronounced as two: hour, fire, tired; I sometimes accent or give them a dieresis, either hoùr or fïre. In New England speech words like prayèr, thère, are apt to be pronounced as two syllables—closer to Elizabethan usage (as with words like gotten) than is modern speech in Britain.

What I notice in practically all editions of Shakespeare's plays is that the editors cannot be relied on to put the accents in the right places. One play edited by a well known Shakespearean editor had, I observed, a dozen accents placed over the wrong syllables. This is understandable, for these people don't write poetry and do not know how to scan. William Shakespeare knew all about scanning, and you need to be both familiar with Elizabethan usage and a practising traditional poet to be able to follow him.

His earlier verse was fairly regular in scansion, mostly iambic pentameter with a great deal of rhyme. As time went on he loosened out, until there are numerous irregular lines—this leaves us much freer in the matter of modernising. Our equivalents should be rhythmically as close as possible, but a strait-jacket need be no part of the equipment. A good Shakespearean scholar tells us, 'there is no necessity for Shakespeare's lines to scan absolutely. He thought of his verse as spoken rather than written and of his rhythmic units in terms of the voice rather than the page.'

There is nothing exclusive or mandatory about my project. We can all read Shakespeare in any edition we like— in the rebarbative olde Englishe spelling of the First Folio, if we wish. Any number of conventional academic editions exist, all weighed down with a burden of notes, many of them superfluous. I propose to make most of them unnecessary—only one occasionally at the foot of very few pages. Let the text be freed of superfluous difficulties, remove obstacles to let it speak for itself, while adhering conservatively to every line.

We really do not need any more editions of the Plays on conventional lines—more than enough of those exist already. But *A Contemporary Shakespeare* on these lines—both revolutionary and conservative—should be a help to everybody all round the world—though especially for younger people, increasingly with time moving away from the language of 400 years ago.

INTRODUCTION

All's Well That Ends Well is a remarkable play from several points of view, and yet—as Professor C. J. Sisson says—it has 'suffered at the hands of critics', who have not perceived its points or how revealing it is. 'In general, the play has been greatly under-rated, not least as an acting play', with its magnificent *dénouement*. Yet it has splendid character parts: Parolles, whom Charles I noted as outstanding in his copy of the Second Folio, one of Shakespeare's most individual comic creations; the Countess of Rossillion, whom Bernard Shaw regarded as 'the most beautiful old woman's part ever written'; her son, the spoiled young aristocrat whom nobody loves— except Helena, the doctor's lower-class daughter; Helena herself, who wins him to her bed if not to her love by the well-known bed-trick, which was welcome to Elizabethan taste if not to ours.

In short, failure to appreciate the play is in part due to the change of taste and values since Shakespeare's day; and with no play is it more important to put it, and see it, in the perspective of its time. Then to interpret it—the proper, and modest, role of critics.

The story came from Boccaccio via Painter's *Palace of Pleasure* (1566). That provided the theme; but, as was Shakespeare's way, it was one that was very relevant to the circumstances of the time and released what he had it in mind to say about them. Crucial to the plot is the sickness of the King, well-nigh fatal, but miraculously cured by a dead doctor's daughter outside the sphere of regular orthodox physicians. She is virtually an empiric—and the conflict between the College of Physicians (referred to as such) and empirics was a topical theme, as we know from Simon Forman's case.[1] Sickness was much in the air: the ageing Queen was moving towards her end in these years 1601–3. Again, as Sisson points out, 'many a royal ward in those days had reason to rebel against his or her disposal in marriage for the benefit of their guardians.' Thus the young Count's 'conduct is natural enough in real Elizabethan life and society.' This historical comment is very helpful to understanding Count Bertram, the character most in need of sympathy—though modern taste would sympathise with him rather than with Helena, the virgin who virtually forces herself upon him.

Where have we met this imbroglio before?—In the case of Shakespeare's young patron, the Earl of Southampton, in which he was closely involved. The spoiled young Earl would not marry—in spite of his duty to his house and the urgent persuasions of his friends. It would seem that Shakespeare's in the Sonnets were not disagreeable to the Countess, his mother, who received a tribute in them. Rather than marry, he preferred to fling off to serve in France, as Bertram does to Italy—both, be it noted, as Generals of Horse, though the King thought it 'a charge too heavy', exactly as the Queen thought in Southampton's case in Ireland. The Earl incurred her displeasure, as the Count did the King's. Both young men served bravely and were wounded.

One hardly needs to go further. In these years, 1601–3, Southampton was languishing sick in the Tower; and 1603

---

[1] cf. my *Simon Forman: Sex and Society in Shakespeare's Age.*

was a bad plague year. In Ireland he was on very familiar terms with a braggadoccio Captain Piers Edmonds, 'culling' him in his arms in his tent. We note that Count Bertram's familiar, the braggart captain Parolles, calls him 'sweetheart'.

A great deal of the time is in this play: we should date it to 1602, the last year of the Queen's life. Pertinent reflections occur on the new and disillusioning society opening out with the new century, the vulgarity of the Jacobean age— the heroic days over—the conflicts of generations and class. Count Bertram is affronted at being married off to a doctor's daughter. The dramatist's comment on that is:

> From lowest place when virtuous things proceed,
> The place is dignified by the doer's deed.

And

> Honours thrive
> When rather from our acts we them derive
> Than our foregoers.

The elderly King quotes the young Count's father against the latter's generation: 'Let me not live', he used to say,

> to be the snuff
> Of younger spirits, whose apprehensive senses
> All but new things disdain; whose judgements are
> Mere fathers of their garments; whose constancies
> Expire before their fashions.

The Countess appeals to the King to pardon her son's injurious conduct on the ground of his youth—which was Southampton's mother's plea on behalf of her son for his rebellion:

Natural rebellion done in the blade of youth,
When oil and fire, too strong for reason's force,
O'erbear it and burn on.

Southampton's rebellion was in the immediate background, in 1601, only a year or two before the play.

We have reason to note again and again Shakespeare's reflections on 'honour', and his constant interest in monuments and tombs—personally characteristic. The mere word 'honour' is

Debauched on every tomb, on every grave
A lying trophy, and as oft is dumb
Where dust and damned oblivion is the tomb
Of honoured bones indeed.

We detect too the sceptical note characteristic of him, since it is so often sounded throughout the plays: 'They say miracles are past, and we have our philosophical persons to make modern [i.e. normal] and familiar things supernatural and causeless. Hence is it that we make trifles of terrors, ensconcing ourselves into seeming knowledge when we should submit ourselves to an unknown fear.' And for a philosophic reflection of his own, unmistakable for all the absurd assumption that we cannot tell what Shakespeare thought himself, when it occurs in different guises again and again: 'The web of our life is of a mingled yarn, good and ill together. Our virtues would be proud if our faults whipped them not, and our crimes would despair if they were not cherished by our virtues.'

We see the application of this tolerant scepticism in experience: 'for young Charbon the Puritan and old Poysam the Papist, howsoever their hearts are severed in religion, their heads are both one: they may jowl horns together like any deer in the herd', i.e. both may be equally cuckolds.

And, we may add, we see the writer's enthusiasm for deer-hunting from early days in everything he wrote. Not much bawdy in this serious play, though he takes an opportunity when it presents itself, and there are the almost regulation references to 'French crowns' and balding from venereal disease, rife in Elizabethan London.

Imperceptive critics are apt to dismiss the rhymed couplets in which he expressed his *sententiae* as 'old-fashioned fustian': but they are characteristic of the age, and ubiquitous in the country: evidently considered appropriate to the thought, like a motto, or indeed the injunction on his gravestone.

> Oft expectation fails, and most of there
> Where most it promises, and oft it hits
> Where hope is coldest and despair most fits.

The language of this play offers no particular difficulties. But a modern edition, which modernises spelling and punctuation—as many sensibly do nowadays—should not keep pointless archaisms like 'vild' for vile, 'yond' for yon. Shakespeare often uses 'in' for words where we should use un, e.g. incertain, inaidable, for uncertain, unaidable; or again, he will use 'un' where the modern usage is in. No sacrosanctity attaches to inconsistency: we are free to modernise. And it is a sheer bonus, in a modern edition, to get rid of such tongue-twisters as 'methink*st* t*h*ou', 'should*st* s*t*rive', 'may*st* t*h*ou', 'should*st* c*h*oose', etc.

Though less popular than it deserves, this play—along with its companion piece, *Measure for Measure*—is of special interest philosophically, provoking thought and telling us what Shakespeare thought.

CHARACTERS

BERTRAM, Count of Rossillion
The COUNTESS of Rossillion, Bertram's mother
HELENA, a young girl brought up by the Countess
PAROLLES, Bertram's follower
Rinaldo, STEWARD in the Countess's household
Lavatch, CLOWN in the Countess's household
A Page
The KING of France
LAFEW, an old Lord
The brothers Dumaine, two French LORDS: later Captains
    serving the Duke of Florence
A GENTLEMAN, Astringer to the Court of France
The DUKE of Florence
A WIDOW of Florence
DIANA, the Widow's daughter
MARIANA, a friend of the Widow

LORDS, ATTENDANTS, SOLDIERS, CITIZENS, French and
    Florentine

18

Act I

SCENE I
The Countess's house.

Enter Bertram, Count of Rossillion, his mother
the Countess, Helena, and Lord Lafew; all in black

COUNTESS   In delivering my son from me, I bury a second
husband.

BERTRAM   And I in going, madam, weep over my father's
death anew; but I must attend his majesty's command,
to whom I am now in ward, evermore in subjection.

LAFEW   You shall find of the King a husband, madam;
you, sir, a father. He that so generally is at all times
good must of necessity hold his virtue to you, whose
worthiness would stir it up where it wanted, rather
than lack it where there is such abundance.

COUNTESS   What hope is there of his majesty's
amendment?

LAFEW   He has abandoned his physicians, madam, under
whose practices he has persecuted time with hope, and
finds no other advantage in the process but only the
losing of hope by time.

COUNTESS   This young gentlewoman had a father—O
that 'had', how sad a passage it is!—whose skill was
almost as great as his honesty; had it stretched so far,
would have made nature immortal, and death should
have play for lack of work. Would for the King's sake he
were living! I think it would be the death of the King's
disease.

LAFEW   How called you the man you speak of, madam?

COUNTESS   He was famous, sir, in his profession, and it
    was his great right to be so: Gerard de Narbonne.

LAFEW   He was excellent indeed, madam. The King very
    lately spoke of him admiringly, and mourningly. He
    was skilful enough to have lived still, if knowledge
    could be set up against mortality.

BERTRAM   What is it, my good lord, the King languishes
    of?

LAFEW   A fistula, my lord.

BERTRAM   I heard not of it before.

LAFEW   I would it were not notorious. Was this gentlewo-
    man the daughter of Gerard de Narbonne?

COUNTESS   His sole child, my lord, and bequeathed to
    my overlooking. I have those hopes of her good, that her
    education promises her disposition she inherits—which
    makes fair gifts fairer. For where an unclean mind carries
    virtuous qualities, there commendations go with pity:
    they are virtues and traitors too. In her they are the
    better for their simpleness. She derives her honesty and
    achieves her goodness.

LAFEW   Your commendations, madam, get from her tears.

COUNTESS   It is the best brine a maiden can season
    her praise in. The remembrance of her father never
    approaches her heart but the tyranny of her sorrows
    takes all livelihood from her cheek. No more of this,
    Helena; go to, no more, lest it be rather thought you
    affect a sorrow than to have it.

HELENA   I do affect a sorrow indeed, but I have it too.

LAFEW   Moderate lamentation is the right of the dead,
    excessive grief the enemy to the living.

COUNTESS   If the living is enemy to the grief, the excess
    makes it soon mortal.

BERTRAM   Madam, I desire your holy wishes.

LAFEW   How understand we that?

COUNTESS
   Be you blessed, Bertram, and succeed your father
   In manners as in shape! Your blood and virtue
   Contend for empire in you, and your goodness
   Share with your birthright! Love all, trust a few,
   Do wrong to none. Be able for your enemy
   Rather in power than use, and keep your friend
   Under your own life's key. Be checked for silence,
   But never taxed for speech. What heaven more will,
   That you may furnish and my prayers pluck down,
   Fall on your head! Farewell.—My lord,
   He is an unseasoned courtier: good my lord,
   Advise him.
LAFEW   He cannot want the best
   That shall attend his love.
COUNTESS   Heaven bless him! Farewell, Bertram.   *Exit*
BERTRAM   The best wishes that can be forged in your
   thoughts be servants to you! (*To Helena*) Be comfortable
   to my mother, your mistress, and make much of her.
LAFEW   Farewell, pretty lady. You must hold the credit of
   your father.   *Exeunt Bertram and Lafew*
HELENA
   O, were that all! I think not on my father,
   And these great tears grace his remembrance more
   Than those I shed for him. What was he like?
   I have forgotten him. My imagination
   Carries no features in it but Bertram's.
   I am undone: there is no living, none,
   If Bertram is away. It were all one
   That I should love a bright particular star
   And think to wed it, he is so above me.
   In his bright radiance and collateral light
   Must I be comforted, not in his sphere.
   The ambition in my love thus plagues itself:
   The hind that would be mated by the lion
   Must die for love. It was pretty, though a plague,

To see him every hour, to sit and draw
His archèd brows, his hawking eye, his curls,
In our heart's table—heart too capable
Of every line and trick of his sweet looks.
But now he's gone, and my idolatrous fancy
Must sanctify his relics. Who comes here?

Enter Parolles

One that goes with him. I love him for his sake,
And yet I know him a notorious liar,
Think him a great way fool, solely a coward;
Yet these fixed evils sit so fit in him
That they take place when virtue's steely bones
Look bleak in the cold wind. Full oft we see
Cold wisdom waiting on superfluous folly.

PAROLLES   Save you, fair queen!

HELENA   And you, monarch!

PAROLLES   No.

HELENA   And no.

PAROLLES   Are you meditating on virginity?

HELENA   Ay. You have some stain of soldier in you: let
me ask you a question. Man is enemy to virginity; how
may we barricade it against him?

PAROLLES   Keep him out.

HELENA   But he assails, and our virginity, though valiant,
in the defence yet is weak. Unfold to us some warlike
resistance.

PAROLLES   There is none. Man setting down before you
will undermine you and blow you up.

HELENA   Bless our poor virginity from underminers and
blowers-up! Is there no military policy how virgins
might blow up men?

PAROLLES   Virginity being blown down, man will quicklier
be blown up; indeed, in blowing him down again, with
the breach yourselves made you lose your city. It is not

politic in the commonwealth of nature to preserve
virginity. Loss of virginity is rational increase, and
there was never virgin got till virginity was first lost.
That you were made of is mettle to make virgins.
Virginity, by being once lost, may be ten times found;
by being ever kept it is ever lost. It is too cold a
companion. Away with it!

HELENA   I will stand for it a little, though therefore I die
a virgin.

PAROLLES   There's little can be said in it; it is against
the rule of nature. To speak on the part of virginity
is to accuse your mothers, which is most infallible
disobedience. He that hangs himself is a virgin; virginity
murders itself, and should be buried in highways out of
all sanctified limit, as a desperate offendress against
nature. Virginity breeds mites, much like a cheese,
consumes itself to the very paring, and so dies with
feeding its own stomach. Besides, virginity is peevish,
proud, idle, made of self-love which is the most inhibited
sin in the canon. Keep it not; you cannot choose but lose
by it. Out with it! Within ten years it will make itself
two, which is a goodly increase, and the principal itself
not much the worse. Away with it!

HELENA   How might one do, sir, to lose it to her own
liking?

PAROLLES   Let me see. Sure, ill, to like him that never it
likes. It is a commodity will lose the gloss with lying;
the longer kept, the less worth. Off with it while it is
vendible; answer the time of request. Virginity, like an
old courtier, wears her cap out of fashion, richly suited
but unsuitable, just like the brooch and the toothpick,
which wear not now. Your date is better in your pie and
your porridge than in your cheek; and your virginity,
your old virginity, is like one of our French withered
pears: it looks ill, it eats drily; to be sure, 'tis a withered
pear; it was formerly better; yet 'tis a withered pear. Will
you anything with it?

HELENA

　　Not my virginity, yet . . .
　　There shall your master have a thousand loves,
　　A mother, and a mistress, and a friend,
　　A phoenix, captain, and an enemy,
　　A guide, a goddess, and a sovereign,
　　A counsellor, a traitress, and a dear.
　　His humble ambition, proud humility,
　　His jarring concord, and his discord dulcet,
　　His faith, his sweet disaster; with a world
　　Of pretty, vain, adopted names when blind
　　Cupid is god-parent. Now shall he—
　　I know not what he shall. God send him well!
　　The Court's a learning-place, and he is one—

PAROLLES

　　What one, in faith?

HELENA

　　That I wish well. It is pity—

PAROLLES

　　What is a pity?

HELENA

　　That wishing well had not a body in it
　　Which might be felt: that we, the poorer born,
　　Whose baser stars do shut us up in wishes,
　　Might with effects of them follow our friends,
　　And show what we alone must think, which never
　　Returns us thanks.

Enter Page

PAGE　Monsieur Parolles, my lord calls for you.　　*Exit*
PAROLLES　Little Helen, farewell. If I can remember you I
　　will think of you at Court.
HELENA　Monsieur Parolles, you were born under a
　　charitable star.

PAROLLES   Under Mars, I.

HELENA   I especially think under Mars.

PAROLLES   Why under Mars?

HELENA   The wars have so kept you under that you must
   needs be born under Mars.

PAROLLES   When he was predominant.

HELENA   When he was retrograde, I think rather.

PAROLLES   Why think you so?

HELENA   You go so much backward when you fight.

PAROLLES   That's for advantage.

HELENA   So is running away, when fear proposes the
   safety. But the composition that your valour and fear
   make in you is a virtue of a good wing, and I like the
   wear well.

PAROLLES   I am so full of businesses I cannot answer you
   acutely. I will return perfect courtier, in which my
   instruction shall serve to naturalize you, so you will be
   capable of a courtier's counsel, and understand what
   advice shall thrust upon you. Else you die in your
   unthankfulness, and your ignorance makes you away.
   Farewell. When you have leisure, say your prayers; when
   you have none, remember your friends. Get you a good
   husband, and use him as he uses you. So, farewell. *Exit*

HELENA
   Our remedies oft in ourselves do lie,
   Which we ascribe to heaven. The fated sky
   Gives us free scope, only does backward pull
   Our slow designs when we ourselves are dull.
   What power is it which mounts my love so high,
   That makes me see, and cannot feed my eye?
   The mightiest space in fortune nature brings
   To join like likes, and kiss like native things.
   Impossible are strange attempts to those
   That weigh their pains in sense, and do suppose
   What has been cannot be. Who ever strove
   To show her merit that did miss her love?

The King's disease—my project may deceive me,
But my intents are fixed, and will not leave me.   *Exit*

SCENE II
The King's palace.

*Flourish of cornets. Enter the King of France with letters,
and attendants*

KING
    The Florentines and Senoys [Siennese] are by the ears,
    Have fought with equal fortune, and continue
    A braving war.
FIRST LORD   So it is reported, sir.
KING
    Nay, it is most credible. We here receive it
    A certainty, vouched from our cousin Austria,
    With caution that the Florentine will move us
    For speedy aid. Wherein our dearest friend
    Prejudicates the business, and would seem
    To have us make denial.
FIRST LORD   His love and wisdom,
    Approved so to your majesty, may plead
    For amplest credence.
KING   He has armed our answer,
    And Florence is denied before he comes.
    Yet, for our gentlemen that mean to see
    The Tuscan service, freely have they leave
    To stand on either part.
SECOND LORD   It well may serve
    A nursery to our gentry, who are sick
    For breathing and exploit.
KING   What's he comes here?

Enter Bertram, Lafew, and Parolles

FIRST LORD
    It is the Count Rossillion, my good lord,
    Young Bertram.
KING   Youth, you bear your father's face;
    Frank nature, rather curious than in haste,
    Has well composed you. Your father's moral parts
    May you inherit too! Welcome to Paris.
BERTRAM
    My thanks and duty are your majesty's.
KING
    I would I had that corporal soundness now,
    As when your father and myself in friendship
    First tried our soldiership. He did look far
    Into the service of the time, and was
    Disciped of the bravest. He lasted long,
    But on us both did haggish age steal on,
    And wore us out of act. It much repairs me
    To talk of your good father. In his youth
    He had the wit which I can well observe
    Today in our young lords; but they may jest
    Till their own scorn returns to them unnoted
    Ere they can hide their levity in honour.
    So like a courtier, contempt or bitterness
    Was not in his pride or sharpness. If they were,
    His equal had awaked them, and his honour,
    Clock to itself, knew the true minute when
    Exception bid him speak; and at this time
    His tongue obeyed his hand. Who were below him
    He used as creatures of another place,
    And bowed his eminent top to their low ranks,
    Making them proud of his humility,
    In their poor praise he humbled. Such a man
    Might be a copy to these younger times;
    Which, followed well, would demonstrate them now
    But goers backward.

BERTRAM   His good remembrance, sir,
  Lies richer in your thoughts than on his tomb;
  So in approof lives not his epitaph
  As in your royal speech.
KING
  Would I were with him! He would always say—
  I think I hear him now; his worthy words
  He scattered not in ears, but grafted them
  To grow there and to bear—'Let me not live',
  This his good melancholy oft began
  On the catastrophe and heel of pastime,
  When it was out, 'Let me not live', said he,
  'After my flame lacks oil, to be the snuff
  Of younger spirits, whose apprehensive senses
  All but new things disdain; whose judgements are
  Mere fathers of their garments; whose constancies
  Expire before their fashions.' This he wished.
  I, after him, do after him wish too,
  Since I nor wax nor honey can bring home,
  I quickly were dissolvèd from my hive
  To give some labourers room.
SECOND LORD   You're loved, sir;
  They that least lend it you shall lack you first.
KING
  I fill a place, I know. How long is it, Count,
  Since the physician at your father's died?
  He was much famed.
BERTRAM   Some six months since, my lord.
KING
  If he were living I would try him yet.
  Lend me an arm.—The rest have worn me out
  With several applications; nature and sickness
  Debate it at their leisure. Welcome, Count,
  My son is no dearer.
BERTRAM   Thank your majesty.
                                        Exeunt. Flourish

SCENE III
The Countess's house.

Enter the Countess, her Steward, and Lavatch her Clown

COUNTESS   I will now hear. What say you of this
  gentlewoman?
STEWARD   Madam, the care I have had to even your
  content I wish might be found in the calendar of my
  past endeavours; for then we wound our modesty, and
  make foul the clearness of our deservings, when of
  ourselves we publish them.
COUNTESS   What does this knave here? Get you gone,
  fellow. The complaints I have heard of you I do not all
  believe; it is my slowness that I do not, for I know you
  lack not folly to commit them, and have ability enough
  to make such knaveries yours.
CLOWN   It is not unknown to you, madam, I am a poor
  fellow.
COUNTESS   Well, sir.
CLOWN   No, madam, it is not so well that I am poor,
  though many of the rich are damned; but if I may have
  your ladyship's good will to go to the world, Isbel your
  woman and I will do as we may.
COUNTESS   Will you needs be a beggar?
CLOWN   I do beg your good will in this case.
COUNTESS   In what case?
CLOWN   In Isbel's case and my own. Service is no heritage,
  and I think I shall never have the blessing of God till I
  have issue of my body; for they say bairns are blessings.
COUNTESS   Tell me your reason why you will marry.
CLOWN   My poor body, madam, requires it. I am driven
  on by the flesh, and he must needs go that the devil
  drives.

COUNTESS   Is this all your worship's reason?

CLOWN   Faith, madam, I have other holy reasons, such as they are.

COUNTESS   May the world know them?

CLOWN   I have been, madam, a wicked creature, as you and all flesh and blood are, and indeed I do marry that I may repent.

COUNTESS   Your marriage, sooner than your wickedness.

CLOWN   I am out of friends, madam, and I hope to have friends for my wife's sake.

COUNTESS   Such friends are your enemies, knave.

CLOWN   You are shallow, madam; even great friends, for the knaves come to do that for me which I am aweary of. He that ploughs my land spares my team, and gives me leave to in the crop. If I am his cuckold, he's my drudge. He that comforts my wife is the cherisher of my flesh and blood; he that cherishes my flesh and blood loves my flesh and blood; he that loves my flesh and blood is my friend; *ergo,* he that kisses my wife is my friend. If men could be contented to be what they are, there were no fear in marriage; for young Charbon the puritan and old Poysam the papist, howsoever their hearts are severed in religion, their heads are both one: they may jowl horns together like any deer in the herd.

COUNTESS   Will you ever be a foul-mouthed and calumnious knave?

CLOWN   A prophet I, madam, and I speak the truth the next way:

>   For I the ballad will repeat
>   Which men full true shall find:
>   Your marriage comes by destiny,
>   Your cuckoo sings by kind.

COUNTESS   Get you gone, sir. I'll talk with you more anon.

STEWARD   May it please you, madam, that he bid Helen come to you: of her I am to speak.

COUNTESS   Fellow, tell my gentlewoman I would speak
   with her—Helen, I mean.

CLOWN
                  Was this fair face the cause, said she,
                     Why the Grecians sackèd Troy?
                        Ill done, done ill,
                     Was this King Priam's joy?
                  With that she sighèd as she stood,
                  With that she sighèd as she stood,
                     And gave this sentence then:
                  Among nine bad if one is good,
                  Among nine bad if one is good,
                     There's yet one good in ten.

COUNTESS   What, one good in ten? You corrupt the song,
   fellow.

CLOWN   One good woman in ten, madam, which is a
   purifying of the song. Would God would serve the
   world so all the year! We'd find no fault with the tithe-
   woman if I were the parson. One in ten, said he! If we
   might have a good woman born but one every blazing
   star or at an earthquake, it would mend the lottery well;
   a man may draw his heart out ere he plucks one.

COUNTESS   You'll be gone, sir knave, and do as I command
   you!

CLOWN   That man should be at woman's command, and
   yet no hurt done! Though honesty is no puritan, yet it
   will do no hurt. It will wear the surplice of humility
   over the black gown of a big heart. I am going, forsooth.
   The business is for Helen to come hither.   *Exit*

COUNTESS   Well, now.

STEWARD   I know, madam, you love your gentlewoman
   entirely.

COUNTESS   Faith, I do. Her father bequeathed her to me
   and she herself, without other advantage, may lawfully
   make title to as much love as she finds. There is more

owing her than is paid, and more shall be paid her than
she will demand.

STEWARD   Madam, I was very late more near her
than I think she wished me. Alone she was, and did
communicate to herself her own words to her own ears;
she thought, I dare vow for her, they touched not any
stranger sense. Her matter was, she loved your son.
Fortune, she said, was no goddess, that had put such
difference betwixt their two estates; Love no god, that
would not extend his might only where qualities were
level; Dian no queen of virgins, that would suffer her
poor knight surprised without rescue in the first assault
or ransom afterward. This she delivered in the most
bitter touch of sorrow that ever I heard virgin exclaim
in, which I held my duty speedily to acquaint you with
since, in the loss that may happen, it concerns you
somewhat to know it.

COUNTESS   You have discharged this honestly; keep it to
yourself. Many likelihoods informed me of this before,
which hung so tottering in the balance that I could
neither believe nor misdoubt. Pray you leave me. Stall
this in your bosom, and I thank you for your honest
care. I will speak with you further anon.   *Exit Steward*

Enter Helena

COUNTESS
Even so it was with me when I was young.
    If ever we are nature's, these are ours; this thorn
Does to our rose of youth rightly belong;
    Our blood to us, this to our blood is born.
It is the show and seal of nature's truth,
Where love's strong passion is impressed in youth.
By our remembrances of days foregone,
Such were our faults, or then we thought them none.
Her eye is sick of it; I observe her now.

HELENA
  What is your pleasure, madam?
COUNTESS   You know, Helen,
  I am a mother to you.
HELENA
  My honourable mistress.
COUNTESS   Nay, a mother.
  Why not a mother? When I said 'a mother',
  I thought you saw a serpent. What's in 'mother'
  That you start at it? I say I am your mother,
  And put you in the catalogue of those
  That were enwombèd mine. It is often seen
  Adoption strives with nature, and choice breeds
  A native slip to us from foreign seeds.
  You never oppressed me with a mother's groan,
  Yet I express to you a mother's care.
  God's mercy, maiden! Does it curd your blood
  To say I am your mother? What's the matter,
  That this distempered messenger of wet,
  The many-coloured Iris, rounds your eye?
  Why, that you are my daughter?
HELENA   That I am not.
COUNTESS
  I say I am your mother.
HELENA   Pardon, madam.
  The Count Rossillion cannot be my brother.
  I am from humble, he from honoured name;
  No note upon my parents, his all noble.
  My master, my dear lord he is, and I
  His servant live, and will his vassal die.
  He must not be my brother.
COUNTESS   Nor I your mother?
HELENA
  You are my mother, madam; would you were—
  So that my lord your son were not my brother—
  Indeed my mother! Or were you both our mothers

I care no more for than I do for heaven,
So I were not his sister. Can it no other
But, I your daughter, he must be my brother?

COUNTESS
Yes, Helen, you might be my daughter-in-law.
God shield you mean it not! 'Daughter' and 'mother'
So strive upon your pulse. What, pale again?
My fear has caught your folly. Now I see
The mystery of your loneliness, and find
Your salt tears' head. Now to all sense 'tis clear:
You love my son. Invention is ashamed
Against the proclamation of your passion
To say you do not. Therefore tell me true;
But tell me then, 'tis so; for, look, your cheeks
Confess it the one to the other, and your eyes
See it so grossly shown in your behaviour
That in their kind they speak it; only sin
And hellish obstinacy tie your tongue,
That truth should be suspected. Speak, is it so?
If it is so, you have wound a goodly clew;
If it is not, forswear it; however, I charge you,
As heaven shall work in me for your avail,
To tell me truly.

HELENA   Good madam, pardon me.

COUNTESS
Do you love my son?

HELENA   Your pardon, noble mistress.

COUNTESS
Love you my son?

HELENA   Do not you love him, madam?

COUNTESS
Do not evade; my love has in it a bond
Whereof the world takes note. Come, come, disclose
The state of your affection, for your passions
Have to the full betrayed you.

HELENA   Then I confess,
 Here on my knee, before high heaven and you,
 That before you, and next unto high heaven,
 I love your son.
 My friends were poor, but honest; so is my love.
 Be not offended, for it hurts not him
 That he is loved of me. I follow him not
 By any token of presumptuous suit,
 Nor would I have him till I do deserve him,
 Yet never know how that desert should be.
 I know I love in vain, strive against hope,
 Yet in this captious and untenable sieve
 I still pour in the waters of my love
 And lack not to lose still. Thus, Indian-like,
 Religious in my error, I adore
 The sun that looks upon its worshipper
 But knows of him no more. My dearest madam,
 Let not your hate encounter with my love,
 For loving where you do; but if yourself,
 Whose agèd honour cites a virtuous youth,
 Did ever, in so true a flame of liking,
 Wish chastely and love dearly, that your Dian
 Was both herself and love—O then, give pity
 To her whose state is such that cannot choose
 But lend and give where she is sure to lose;
 That seeks not to find what her search implies,
 But riddle-like lives sweetly where she dies.

COUNTESS
 Had you not lately an intent—speak truly—
 To go to Paris?

HELENA   Madam, I had.

COUNTESS   Wherefore? tell true.

HELENA
 I will tell truth, by grace itself I swear.
 You know my father left me some prescriptions
 Of rare and proved effects, such as his reading
 And manifest experience had collected

For general sovereignty. And that he willed me
In heedfullest reservation to bestow them,
As notes whose faculties inclusive were
More than they were reported. Among the rest
There is a remedy, approved, set down,
To cure the desperate languishings whereof
The King is rendered lost.

COUNTESS   This was your motive
For Paris, was it? Speak.

HELENA
My lord your son made me to think of this,
Else Paris and the medicine and the King
Had from the conversation of my thoughts
Haply been absent then.

COUNTESS   But think you, Helen,
If you should tender your supposèd aid,
He would receive it? He and his physicians
Are of a mind: he, that they cannot help him;
They, that they cannot help. How shall they credit
A poor unlearnèd virgin, when the schools,
Embowelled of their doctrine, have left off
The danger to itself?

HELENA   There's something in it
More than my father's skill, which was the greatest
Of his profession, that his good receipt
Shall for my legacy be sanctified
By the luckiest stars in heaven. And would your honour
But give me leave to try success, I'd venture
The well-lost life of mine on his grace's cure
By such a day, and hour.

COUNTESS   Do you believe it?

HELENA
Ay, madam, knowingly.

COUNTESS
Why, Helen, you shall have my leave and love,
Means and attendants, and my loving greetings

To those of mine in Court. I'll stay at home
And pray God's blessing into your attempt.
Be gone tomorrow, and be sure of this,
What I can help you to, you shall not miss.   *Exeunt*

Act II

SCENE I
The King's Palace.

Enter the King with Lords; Bertram and Parolles;
attendants. Flourish of cornets

KING
    Farewell, young lords; these warlike principles
    Do not throw from you; and you, my lords, farewell.
    Share the advice between you; if both gain all,
    The gift does stretch itself as it is received,
    And is enough for both.

FIRST LORD   It is our hope, sir,
    As experienced soldiers, to return
    And find your grace in health.

KING
    No, no, it cannot be; and yet my heart
    Will not confess it owns the malady
    That does my life besiege. Farewell, young lords.
    Whether I live or die, be you the sons
    Of worthy Frenchmen. Let higher Italy—
    Except those that inherit but the fall
    Of the last monarchy—see that you come
    Not to woo honour, but to wed it. When
    The bravest seeker shrinks, find what you seek,
    That fame may cry you loud. I say farewell.

FIRST LORD
    Health at your bidding serve your majesty!

KING

    Those girls of Italy, take heed of them:

    They say our French lack language to deny

    If they demand. Beware of being captives

    Before you serve.

BOTH LORDS   Our hearts receive your warnings.

KING

    Farewell. *(To some attendants)* Come hither to me.

He withdraws

FIRST LORD

    O my sweet lord, that you will stay behind us!

PAROLLES

    'Tis not his fault, the spark.

SECOND LORD   O, 'tis brave wars!

PAROLLES

    Most wonderful! I have seen those wars.

BERTRAM

    I am commanded here, frustrated with

    'Too young', and 'The next year', and ''Tis too early'.

PAROLLES

    If your mind stands to it, boy, steal away bravely.

BERTRAM

    I shall stay here the forehorse to a smock,

    Creaking my shoes on the plain masonry,

    Till honour is bought up, and no sword worn

    But one to dance with. By heaven, I'll steal away!

FIRST LORD

    There's honour in the theft.

PAROLLES   Commit it, Count.

SECOND LORD   I am your accessary; and so farewell.

BERTRAM   I grow to you, and our parting is a tortured body.

FIRST LORD   Farewell, captain.

SECOND LORD   Sweet Monsieur Parolles!

PAROLLES   Noble heroes, my sword and yours are kin.
Good sparks and lustrous, a word, good metals. You
shall find in the regiment of the Spinii one Captain
Spurio, with his scar, an emblem of war, here on his
sinister cheek; it was this very sword entrenched it. Say
to him I live, and observe his reports for me.

FIRST LORD   We shall, noble captain.   *Exeunt the Lords*

PAROLLES   Mars dote on you for his novices! *(To Bertram)*
What will you do?

BERTRAM   Stay: the King.

PAROLLES   Use a more spacious ceremony to the noble
lords; you have restrained yourself within the list of too
cold an adieu. Be more expressive to them, for they wear
themselves in the cap of the time; there do muster true
gait, eat, speak, and move, under the influence of the
most received star; and though the devil leads the
measure, such are to be followed. After them, and take a
more dilated farewell.

BERTRAM   And I will do so.

PAROLLES   Worthy fellows, and like to prove most sinewy
sword-men.   *Exeunt Bertram and Parolles*

Enter Lafew. The King comes forward

LAFEW   *(kneeling)*
Pardon, my lord, for me and for my tidings.

KING
I'll sue you to stand up.

LAFEW
Then here's a man stands that has brought his pardon,
I would you had kneeled, my lord, to ask me mercy,
And that at my bidding you could so stand up.

KING
I would I had, so I had broken your pate
And asked you mercy for it.

LAFEW   Good faith, a hit!
    But, my good lord, 'tis thus: will you be cured
    Of your infirmity?

KING   No.

LAFEW   O, will you eat
    No grapes, my royal fox? Yes, but you will
    My noble grapes, and if my royal fox
    Could reach them. I have seen a medicine
    That is able to breathe life into a stone,
    Quicken a rock, and make you dance canary
    With sprightly fire and motion; whose simple touch
    Is powerful to araise King Pepin, nay,
    To give great Charlemagne a pen in his hand
    And write to her a love-line.

KING   What 'her' is this?

LAFEW

    Why, Doctor She! My lord, there's one arrived,
    If you will see her. Now by my faith and honour—
    If seriously I may convey my thoughts
    In this my light deliverance—I have spoken
    With one that in her sex, her years, profession,
    Wisdom, and constancy has amazed me more
    Than I dare blame my weakness. Will you see her,
    For that is her demand, and know her business?
    That done, laugh well at me.

KING   Now, good Lafew,
    Bring in the wonderment, that we with you
    May spend our wonder too, or take off yours
    By wondering how you took it.

LAFEW   Nay, I'll show you,
    And not be all day either.

KING
    Thus he his special nothing ever prologues.

LAFEW
    Nay, come your ways.

Enter Helena

KING   This haste has wings indeed.
LAFEW
   Nay, come your ways.
   This is his majesty: say your mind to him.
   A traitor you do look like, but such traitors
   His majesty seldom fears. I am Cressid's uncle
   That dare leave two together. Fare you well.   *Exit*
KING
   Now, fair one, does your business follow us?
HELENA
   Ay, my good lord.
   Gerard de Narbonne was my father,
   In what he did profess, well found.
KING   I knew him.
HELENA
   The rather will I spare my praises towards him;
   Knowing him is enough. On his bed of death
   Many receipts he gave me; chiefly one,
   Which, as the dearest issue of his practice,
   And of his old experience the only darling,
   He bade me store up as a triple eye,
   Safer than my own two, more dear. I have so,
   And hearing your high majesty is touched
   With that malignant cause wherein the honour
   Of my dear father's gift stands chief in power,
   I come to tender it and my appliance,
   With all bound humbleness.
KING   We thank you, maiden,
   But may not be so credulous of cure,
   When our most learnèd doctors leave us, and
   The congregated college have concluded
   That labouring art can never ransom nature
   From her unaidible estate. I say we must not
   So stain our judgement or corrupt our hope,
   To prostitute our past-cure malady

To empirics, or to dissever so
Our great self and our credit, to esteem
A senseless help, when help past sense we deem.

HELENA

My duty then shall pay me for my pains.
I will no more enforce my office on you,
Humbly entreating from your royal thoughts
A modest one to bear me back again.

KING

I cannot give you less, to be called grateful.
You thought to help me, and such thanks I give
As one near death to those that wish him live.
But what at full I know, you know no part;
I knowing all my peril, you no art.

HELENA

What I can do can do no hurt to try,
Since you set up your stand against remedy.
He that of greatest works is finisher
Oft does them by the weakest minister.
So holy writ in babes has judgement shown,
When judges have been babes; great floods have flown
From simple sources; and great seas have dried
When miracles have by the greatest been denied.
Oft expectation fails, and most oft there
Where most it promises, and oft it hits
Where hope is coldest and despair most fits.

KING

I must not hear you. Fare you well, kind maid.
Your pains, not used, must by yourself be paid;
Proffers not taken reap thanks for their reward.

HELENA

Inspirèd merit so by breath is barred.
It is not so with Him that all things knows
As it is with us that base our guess on shows;
But most it is presumption in us when
The help of heaven we count the act of men.

Dear sir, to my endeavours give consent.
Of heaven, not me, make an experiment.
I am not an impostor, that proclaim
Myself against the level of my aim,
But know I think, and think I know most sure,
My art is not past power, nor you past cure.

KING

Are you so confident? Within what space
Hope you my cure?

HELENA   The greatest grace lending grace,
Ere twice the horses of the sun shall bring
Their fiery torcher his diurnal ring,
Ere twice in murk and occidental damp
Moist Hesperus has quenched her sleepy lamp;
Or four and twenty times the pilot's glass
Has told the thievish minutes how they pass,
What is infirm from your sound parts shall fly,
Health shall live free and sickness freely die.

KING

Upon your certainty and confidence
What dare you venture?

HELENA   Tax of impudence,
A strumpet's boldness, a divulgèd shame;
Traduced by odious ballads my maiden's name;
Seared otherwise, nor worse of worst, extended
With vilest torture let my life be ended.

KING

I think in you some blessèd spirit does speak
His powerful sound within an organ weak;
And what impossibility would slay
In common sense, sense saves another way.
Your life is dear, for all that life can rate
Worth name of life in you has estimate:
Youth, beauty, wisdom, courage—all
That happiness and prime can happy call.
You this to hazard needs must intimate

Skill infinite, or monstrous desperate.
Sweet practiser, your physic I will try,
That ministers your own death if I die.

HELENA

If I break time, or flinch in property
Of what I spoke, unpitied let me die,
And well deserved. Not helping, death is my fee;
But if I help, what do you promise me?

KING

Make your demand.

HELENA   But will you make it even?

KING

Ay, by my sceptre and my hopes of heaven.

HELENA

Then shall you give me with your kingly hand
What husband in your power I will command:
Exempted be from me the arrogance
To choose from forth the royal blood of France
My low and humble name to propagate,
With any branch or image of your state;
But such a one, your vassal, whom I know
Is free for me to ask, you to bestow.

KING

Here is my hand; the premises observed,
Your will by my performance shall be served.
So make the choice of your own time, for I,
Your resolved patient, on you still rely.
More should I question you, and more I must,
Though more to know could not be more to trust:
From whence you came, how tended on—but rest
Unquestioned welcome, and undoubted blessed.
Give me some help here, ho! If you proceed
As high as word, my deed shall match your deed.

Flourish. Exeunt

SCENE II
The Countess's house.

Enter the Countess and the Clown

COUNTESS   Come on, sir. I shall now put you to the
height of your breeding.

CLOWN   I will show myself highly fed and lowly taught.
I know my business is but to the Court.

COUNTESS   To the Court! Why, what place make you
special, when you put off that with such contempt? But
to the Court!

CLOWN   Truly, madam, if God has lent a man any
manners he may easily put it off at Court. He that
cannot make a leg, put off his cap, kiss his hand, and
say nothing, has neither leg, hands, lip, nor cap; and
indeed such a fellow, to say precisely, were not for the
Court. But for me, I have an answer will serve all men.

COUNTESS   Indeed, that's a bountiful answer that fits all
questions.

CLOWN   It is like a barber's chair that fits all buttocks:
the pin-buttock, the squat-buttock, the brawn-buttock,
or any buttock.

COUNTESS   Will your answer serve fit to all questions?

CLOWN   As fit as ten groats is for the hand of an attorney,
as your French crown for your taffeta whore, as Tib's
rush ring for Tom's forefinger; as a pancake for Shrove
Tuesday, a morris for May-day, as the nail to its hole,
the cuckold to his horn; as a scolding quean to a
wrangling knave, as the nun's lip to the friar's mouth;
nay, as the pudding to its skin.

COUNTESS   Have you, I say, an answer of such fitness for
all questions?

CLOWN   From below your duke to beneath your constable,
it will fit any question.

COUNTESS   It must be an answer of most monstrous size
that must fit all demands.

CLOWN   But a trifle, in good faith, if the learned should
speak truth of it. Here it is, and all that belongs to it.
Ask me if I am a courtier; it shall do you no harm to
learn.

COUNTESS   To be young again, if we could! I will be a
fool in question, hoping to be the wiser by your answer.
I pray you, sir, are you a courtier?

CLOWN   O Lord, sir!—There's a simple putting off. More,
more, a hundred of them.

COUNTESS   Sir, I am a poor friend of yours that loves
you.

CLOWN   O Lord, sir!—Quick, quick; spare not me.

COUNTESS   I think, sir, you can eat none of this homely
meat.

CLOWN   O Lord, sir!—Nay, put me to it, I warrant you.

COUNTESS   You were lately whipped, sir, as I think.

CLOWN   O Lord, sir!—Spare not me.

COUNTESS   Do you cry 'O Lord, sir!' at your whipping,
and 'spare not me'? Indeed your 'O Lord, sir!' is very
sequent to your whipping: you would answer very well
to a whipping, if you were but bound to it.

CLOWN   I never had worse luck in my life in my 'O Lord,
sir!' I see things may serve long, but not serve ever.

COUNTESS

I play the noble housewife with the time,

To entertain it so merrily with a fool.

CLOWN

O Lord, sir!—Why, there it serves well again.

COUNTESS

An end, sir! To your business: give Helen this,

And urge her to a present answer back.

Commend me to my kinsmen and my son.

This is not much.

CLOWN   Not much commendation to them?

COUNTESS   Not much employment for you. You understand me?

CLOWN   Most fruitfully. I am there before my legs.

COUNTESS   Haste you again.

Exeunt

SCENE III
The King's palace.

Enter Bertram, Lafew, and Parolles

LAFEW   They say miracles are past, and we have our philosophical persons to make normal and familiar, things supernatural and causeless. Hence is it that we make trifles of terrors, ensconcing ourselves into seeming knowledge when we should submit ourselves to an unknown fear.

PAROLLES   Why, 'tis the rarest argument of wonder that has shot out in our latter times.

BERTRAM   And so it is.

LAFEW   To be relinquished of the artists—

PAROLLES   So I say—both of Galen and Paracelsus.

LAFEW   Of all the learnèd and authentic fellows—

PAROLLES   Right, so I say.

LAFEW   That gave him out incurable—

PAROLLES   Why, there it is, so say I too.

LAFEW   Not to be helped.

PAROLLES   Right, as it were a man assured of a—

LAFEW   Uncertain life and sure death.

PAROLLES   Just, you say well. So would I have said.

LAFEW   I may truly say it is a novelty to the world.

PAROLLES   It is indeed. If you will have it in showing, you shall read it in what-do-you-call there.

LAFEW   A showing of a heavenly effect in an earthly actor.

PAROLLES   That's it, I would have said the very same.

LAFEW   Why, your dolphin is not lustier. Before me, I speak in respect—

PAROLLES   Nay, 'tis strange, 'tis very strange, that is the brief and the tedious of it; and he's of a most villainous spirit that will not acknowledge it to be the—

LAFEW   Very hand of heaven.

PAROLLES   Ay, so I say.

LAFEW   In a most weak—

PAROLLES   And feeble minister, great power, great transcendence, which should indeed give us a further use to be made than alone the recovery of the King, as to be—

LAFEW   Generally thankful.

Enter the King, Helena, and attendants

PAROLLES   I would have said it, you say well. Here comes the King.

LAFEW   Lustig, as the German says. I'll like a maid the better while I have a tooth in my head. Why, he's able to lead her a coranto [a dance].

PAROLLES   *Mor du vinager!* Is not this Helen?

LAFEW   Before God, I think so.

KING
    Go, call before me all the lords in Court.
                                    Exit an attendant
    Sit, my preserver, by your patient's side,
    And with this healthful hand, whose banished sense
    You have recalled, a second time receive
    The confirmation of my promised gift,
    Which but attends your naming.

Enter four Lords

Fair maid, send forth your eye. This youthful parcel
Of noble bachelors stand at my bestowing,
Over whom both sovereign power and father's voice
I have to use. Your frank election make;
You have power to choose, and they none to forsake.

HELENA

To each of you one fair and virtuous mistress
Fall, when love pleases! Yet, to each but one!

LAFEW

I'd give my bay horse and his furniture
My mouth no more were broken than these boys',
And claimed as little beard.

KING   Peruse them well.
Not one of those but had a noble father.

HELENA

Gentlemen,
Heaven has through me restored the King to health.

ALL THE LORDS

We understand it, and thank heaven for you.

HELENA

I am a simple maid, and therein wealthiest
That I protest I simply am a maid.
Please it your majesty, I have done already.
The blushes in my cheeks thus whisper me:
'We blush that you should choose, but, be refused,
Let the white death sit on your cheek for ever,
We'll never come there again.'

KING   Make choice and see,
Who shuns your love shuns all his love in me.

HELENA

Now, Dian, from your altar do I fly,
And to imperial Love, that god most high,
Do my sighs stream. (*To First Lord*) Sir, will you hear
    my suit?

FIRST LORD
  And grant it.
HELENA   Thanks, sir. All the rest is mute.
LAFEW   I had rather be in this choice than throw an ace
  for my life.
HELENA   (*to Second Lord*)
  The honour, sir, that flames in your fair eyes
  Before I speak, too threateningly replies.
  Love make your fortunes twenty times above
  Her that so wishes, and her humble love!
SECOND LORD
  No better, if you please.
HELENA   My wish receive,
  Which great Love grant. And so I take my leave.
LAFEW Do all they deny her? If they were sons of mine I
  would have them whipped, or I would send them to
  the Turk to make eunuchs of.
HELENA   (*to Third Lord*)
  Be not afraid that I your hand should take;
  I'll never do you wrong, for your own sake.
  Blessing upon your vows, and in your bed
  Find fairer fortune if you ever wed!
LAFEW   These boys are boys of ice; they'll none have her.
  Sure, they are bastards to the English; the French never
  got them.
HELENA   (*to Fourth Lord*)
  You are too young, too happy, and too good
  To make yourself a son out of my blood.
FOURTH LORD   Fair one, I think not so.
LAFEW   There's one grape yet. I am sure your father drank
  wine; but if you are not an ass, I am a youth of fourteen;
  I have known you already.
HELENA   (*to Bertram*)
  I dare not say I take you, but I give
  Me and my service, ever while I live,
  Into your guiding power. This is the man.

KING
    Why, then, young Bertram, take her, she's your wife.
BERTRAM
    My wife, my lord! I shall beseech your highness,
    In such a business give me leave to use
    The help of my own eyes.
KING   Know you not, Bertram,
    What she has done for me?
BERTRAM   Yes, my good lord,
    But never hope to know why I should marry her.
KING
    You know she has raised me from my sickly bed.
BERTRAM
    But follows it, my lord, to bring me down
    Must answer for your raising? I know her well:
    She had her breeding at my father's charge.
    A poor physician's daughter my wife! Disdain
    Rather corrupt me ever!
KING
    It is only title you disdain in her, which
    I can build up. Strange is it that our bloods,
    Of colour, weight, and heat, poured all together,
    Would quite confound distinction, yet stands off
    In differences so mighty. If she is
    All that is virtuous, save what you dislike—
    A poor physician's daughter—you dislike
    Of virtue for the name. But do not so.
    From lowest place when virtuous things proceed,
    The place is dignified by the doer's deed.
    Where great additions swell us and virtue none,
    It is a dropsied honour. Good alone
    Is good, without a name: vileness is so;
    The property by what it is should go,
    Not by the title. She is young, wise, fair;
    In these to nature she's immediate heir,
    And these breed honour; that is honour's scorn

Which challenges itself as honour's born
And is not like the sire. Honours thrive
When rather from our acts we them derive
Than our foregoers. The mere word's a slave,
Debauched on every tomb, on every grave
A lying trophy, and as oft is dumb
Where dust and damned oblivion are the tomb
Of honoured bones indeed. What should be said?
If you can like this creature as a maid,
I can create the rest. Virtue and she
Are her own dower; honour and wealth from me.

BERTRAM

I cannot love her nor will strive to do it.

KING

You wrong yourself if you should strive to choose.

HELENA

That you are well restored, my lord, I'm glad.
Let the rest go.

KING

My honour's at the stake, which to defeat,
I must produce my power. Here, take her hand,
Proud, scornful boy, unworthy this good gift,
That do in vile contempt so shackle up
My love and her desert; that can not dream
We, poising us in her defective scale,
Shall weigh you to the beam; that will not know
It is in us to plant your honour where
We please to have it grow. Check your contempt.
Obey our will which travails in your good.
Believe not your disdain, but forthrightly
Do your own fortunes that obedient right
Which both your duty owes and our power claims.
Or I will throw you from my care for ever
Into the staggers and the careless lapse
Of youth and ignorance; both my revenge and hate
Loosing upon you in the name of justice,
Without all terms of pity. Speak. Your answer.

BERTRAM
    Pardon, my gracious lord; for I submit
    My fancy to your eyes. When I consider
    What great creation and what share of honour
    Fly where you bid it, I find that she, who late
    Was in my nobler thoughts most base, is now
    The praisèd of the King; who, so ennobled,
    Is as it were born so.

KING   Take her by the hand
    And tell her she is yours; to whom I promise
    A counterpoise, if not to your estate,
    A balance more replete.

BERTRAM   I take her hand.

KING
    Good fortune and the favour of the King
    Smile upon this contract, whose ceremony
    Shall follow swiftly on the new-born brief,
    And be performed tonight. The solemn feast
    Shall more attend upon the coming space,
    Expecting absent friends. As you love her
    Your love's to me religious; else, does err.

                           Exeunt all but Parolles and Lafew

LAFEW   Do you hear, monsieur? A word with you.

PAROLLES   Your pleasure, sir.

LAFEW   Your lord and master did well to make his
recantation.

PAROLLES   Recantation! My lord! My master!

LAFEW   Ay. Is it not a language I speak?

PAROLLES   A most harsh one, and not to be understood
without bloody succeeding. My master!

LAFEW   Are you companion to the Count Rossillion?

PAROLLES   To any Count, to all Counts, to what is man.

LAFEW   To what is Count's man; Count's master is of
another style.

PAROLLES   You are too old, sir; let it satisfy you, you are
   too old.

LAFEW   I must tell you, fellow, I write man, to which title
   age cannot bring you.

PAROLLES   What I dare too well do, I dare not do.

LAFEW   I did think you for two mealtimes to be a pretty
   wise fellow. You did make tolerable vent of your travel;
   it might pass. Yet the scarfs and the bannerets you
   about did manifoldly dissuade me from believing you a
   vessel of too great a burden. I have now found you;
   when I lose you again I care not. Yet are you good for
   nothing but taking up, and that you are scarce worth.

PAROLLES   Had you not the privilege of antiquity upon
   you—

LAFEW   Do not plunge yourself too far in anger, lest you
   hasten your trial; which if—Lord have mercy on you for
   a hen! So, my good window of lattice, fare you well;
   your casement I need not open, for I look through you.
   Give me your hand.

PAROLLES   My lord, you give me most egregious indignity.

LAFEW   Ay, with all my heart; and you are worthy of it.

PAROLLES   I have not, my lord, deserved it.

LAFEW   Yes, good faith, every dram of it, and I will not
   spare you a scruple.

PAROLLES   Well, I shall be wiser.

LAFEW   Even as soon as you can, for you have to drink a
   bellyful of the contrary. If ever you are bound in your
   scarf and beaten, you shall find what it is to be proud of
   your bondage. I have a desire to hold my acquaintance
   with you, or rather my knowledge, that I may say, when
   you default, 'He is a man I know'.

PAROLLES   My lord, you do me most insupportable
   vexation.

LAFEW   I would it were hell-pains for your sake, and my
   poor doing eternal; for doing I am past, as I will by you,
   in what motion age will give me leave.   *Exit*

PAROLLES   Well, you have a son shall take this disgrace
off me, scurvy, old, filthy, scurvy lord! Well, I must be
patient, there is no fettering of authority. I'll beat him,
by my life, if I can meet him with any convenience, if
he were double and double a lord. I'll have no more pity
on his age than I would have on—I'll beat him if I could
but meet him again.

Enter Lafew

LAFEW   Fellow, your lord and master's married, there's
news for you; you have a new mistress.
PAROLLES   I most unfeignedly beseech your lordship to
make some reservation of your wrongs. He is my good
lord: whom I serve above is my master.
LAFEW   Who? God?
PAROLLES   Ay, sir.
LAFEW   The devil it is that's your master. Why do you
garter up your arms in this fashion? Do you make hose
of your sleeves? Do other servants so? You were best set
your lower part where your nose stands. By my honour,
if I were but two hours younger I'd beat you. I think you
are a general offence and every man should beat you. I
think you were created for men to breathe themselves
upon you.
PAROLLES   This is hard and undeserved measure, my lord.
LAFEW   Go to, sir. You were beaten in Italy for picking
a kernel out of a pomegranate. You are a vagabond
and no true traveller. You are more saucy with lords and
honourable personages than the commission of your
birth and virtue gives you heraldry. You are not worth
another word, else I'd call you knave. I leave you.   *Exit*

Enter Bertram

PAROLLES   Good, very good, it is so then. Good, very

good; let it be concealed awhile.

BERTRAM

Undone and forfeited to cares for ever!

PAROLLES   What's the matter, sweetheart?

BERTRAM

Although before the solemn priest I have sworn,
I will not bed her.

PAROLLES

What, what, sweetheart?

BERTRAM

O my Parolles, they have married me!
I'll to the Tuscan wars and never bed her.

PAROLLES

France is a dog-hole and it no more merits
The tread of a man's foot. To the wars!

BERTRAM

There's letters from my mother: what the import is I
know not yet.

PAROLLES

Ay, that would be known. To the wars, my boy, to the
wars!
He wears his honour in a box unseen
That hugs his kicky-wicky here at home,
Spending his manly marrow in her arms,
Who should sustain the bound and high curvet
Of Mars's fiery steed. To other regions!
France is a stable, we that dwell in it, jades.
Therefore to the wars!

BERTRAM

It shall be so. I'll send her to my house,
Acquaint my mother with my hate to her
And wherefore I am fled; write to the King
That which I durst not speak. His present gift
Shall furnish me to those Italian fields
Where noble fellows strike. War is no strife
To the dark house and the detested wife.

PAROLLES
 Will this capriccio hold in you, for sure?
BERTRAM
 Go with me to my chamber and advise me.
 I'll send her straight away. Tomorrow
 I'll to the wars, she to her single sorrow.
PAROLLES
 Why, these balls bound, there's noise in it. 'Tis hard:
 A young man married is a man that's marred.
 Therefore away, and leave her bravely; go.
 The King has done you wrong, but hush, 'tis so.

Exeunt

SCENE IV
The King's Palace.

Enter Helena and the Clown

HELENA   My mother greets me kindly. Is she well?
CLOWN   She is not well, but yet she has her health; she's
 very merry, but yet she is not well. But thanks be given
 she's very well and wants nothing in the world; but yet
 she is not well.
HELENA   If she is very well, what does she ail that she is
 not very well?
CLOWN   Truly, she is very well indeed, but for two things.
HELENA   What two things?
CLOWN   One, that she is not in heaven, whither God
 send her quickly! The other, that she's on earth, from
 whence God send her quickly!

Enter Parolles

PAROLLES   Bless you, my fortunate lady.
HELENA   I hope, sir, I have your good will to have my
 own good fortune.

PAROLLES   You had my prayers to lead them on, and to
    keep them on have them still. O, my knave! How does
    my old lady?

CLOWN   So that you had her wrinkles and I her money, I
    would she did as you say.

PAROLLES   Why, I say nothing.

CLOWN   Well, you are the wiser man, for many a man's
    tongue shakes out his master's undoing. To say nothing,
    to do nothing, to know nothing, and to have nothing, is
    to be a great part of your title, which is within a very
    little of nothing.

PAROLLES   Away! You are a knave.

CLOWN   You should have said, sir, 'Before a knave you
    are a knave'; that's 'Before me, you are a knave'. This
    had been truth, sir.

PAROLLES   Go to, you are a witty fool: I have found you.

CLOWN   Did you find me in your self, sir, or were you
    taught to find me? The search, sir, was profitable; and
    much fool may you find in you, even to the world's
    pleasure and the increase of laughter.

PAROLLES

    A good knave in faith, and well fed.
    Madam, my lord will go away tonight;
    A very serious business calls on him.
    The great prerogative and rite of love,
    Which as your due time claims, he does acknowledge,
    But puts it off to a compelled restraint:
    Whose want and whose delay are strewed with sweets,
    Which they distil now in the curbèd time,
    To make the coming hour o'erflow with joy
    And pleasure drown the brim.

HELENA   What's his will else?

PAROLLES

    That you will take your instant leave of the King,
    And make this haste as your own good proceeding,

Strengthened with what apology you think
May make it probable need.

HELENA   What more commands he?

PAROLLES
That, having this obtained, you immediately
Attend his further pleasure.

HELENA
In everything I wait upon his will.

PAROLLES
I shall report it so.   *Exit*

HELENA
I pray you. Come, boy.   *Exeunt*

SCENE V
The same.

Enter Lafew and Bertram

LAFEW   But I hope your lordship thinks not him a soldier.

BERTRAM   Yes, my lord, and of very valiant proof.

LAFEW   You have it from his own deliverance.

BERTRAM   And by other warranted testimony.

LAFEW   Then my dial goes not true: I took this lark for a
bunting.

BERTRAM   I do assure you, my lord, he is very great in
knowledge, and accordingly valiant.

LAFEW   I have then sinned against his experience and
transgressed against his valour, and my state that way is
dangerous, since I cannot yet find in my heart to repent.
Here he comes. I pray you make us friends; I will pursue
the amity.

Enter Parolles

PAROLLES   *(to Bertram)* These things shall be done, sir.

LAFEW   Pray you, sir, who's his tailor?

PAROLLES   Sir!

LAFEW   O, I know him well. Ay, sir, he, sir, is a good workman, a very good tailor.

BERTRAM   *(aside to Parolles)* Is she gone to the King?

PAROLLES   She is.

BERTRAM   Will she away tonight?

PAROLLES   As you will have her.

BERTRAM

I have written my letters, casketed my treasure,
Given order for our horses; and tonight,
When I should take possession of the bride,
End ere I do begin.

LAFEW   *(aside)*. A good traveller is something at the latter end of a dinner; but one that lies three thirds and uses a known truth to pass a thousand nothings with, should be once heard and thrice beaten. *(Aloud)* God save you, captain!

BERTRAM   Is there any unkindness between my lord and you, monsieur?

PAROLLES   I know not how I have deserved to run into my lord's displeasure.

LAFEW   You have made shift to run into it, boots and spurs and all, like him that leaped into the custard; and out of it you'll run again rather than suffer question for your residence.

BERTRAM   It may be you have mistaken him, my lord.

LAFEW   And shall do so ever, though I took him at his prayers. Fare you well, my lord, and believe this of me: there can be no kernel in this light nut. The soul of this man is his clothes. Trust him not in matter of heavy consequence. I have kept some of them tame, and know their natures. Farewell, monsieur; I have spoken better of you than you have or will to deserve at my hand, but we must do good against evil.   *Exit*

PAROLLES   An idle lord, I swear.

BERTRAM   I think not so.

PAROLLES   Why, do you not know him?

BERTRAM
Yes, I do know him well, and common speech
Gives him a worthy pass. Here comes my clog.

Enter Helena

HELENA
I have, sir, as I was commanded from you,
Spoken with the King, and have procured his leave
For present parting; only he desires
Some private speech with you.

BERTRAM   I shall obey his will.
You must not marvel, Helen, at my course,
Which holds not colour with the time, nor does
The ministration and requirèd office
On my particular. Prepared I was not
For such a business, therefore am I found
So much unsettled. This drives me to entreat you
That now at once you take your way for home,
And rather muse than ask why I entreat you.
For my respects are better than they seem,
And my appointments have in them a need
Greater than shows itself at the first view
To you that know them not. This to my mother.

He gives Helena a letter

It will be two days ere I shall see you, so
I leave you to your wisdom.

HELENA   Sir, I can nothing say
But that I am your most obedient servant.

BERTRAM
Come, come, no more of that.

HELENA   And ever shall
    With true observance seek to eke out that
    Wherein toward me my homely stars have failed
    To equal my great fortune.
BERTRAM   Let that go.
    My haste is very great. Farewell. Hie home.
HELENA
    Pray, sir, your pardon.
BERTRAM   Well, what would you say?
HELENA
    I am not worthy of the wealth I own,
    Nor dare I say 'tis mine—and yet it is;
    But, like a timorous thief, most fain would steal
    What law does vouch my own.
BERTRAM   What would you have?
HELENA
    Something, and scarce so much; nothing indeed.
    I would not tell you what I would, my lord.
    Faith, yes:
    Strangers and foes do sunder and not kiss.
BERTRAM
    I pray you, stay not, but in haste to horse.
HELENA
    I shall not break your bidding, good my lord.
    Where are my other men? Monsieur, farewell.   *Exit*
BERTRAM
    Go you toward home, where I will never come
    While I can shake my sword or hear the drum.
    Away, and for our flight.
PAROLLES   Bravely. Coragio!   *Exeunt*

Act III

SCENE I
The Duke of Florence's Palace.

Flourish. Enter the Duke of Florence, and two French
Lords, with soldiers

DUKE
So that from point to point now have you heard
The fundamental reasons of this war,
Whose great decision has much blood let forth,
And more thirsts after.
FIRST LORD   Holy seems the quarrel
Upon your grace's part, black and fearful
On the opposer.
DUKE
Therefore we marvel much our cousin France
Would in so just a business shut his bosom
Against our borrowing prayers.
SECOND LORD   Good my lord,
The reasons of our state I cannot yield,
But like a common and an outside man
That the great figure of a council frames
By self-unable motion; therefore dare not
Say what I think of it, since I have found
Myself in my uncertain grounds to fail
As often as I guessed.
DUKE   Be it his pleasure.
FIRST LORD
But I am sure the younger of our nature
That surfeit on their ease will day by day

Come here for physic.

DUKE   Welcome shall they be,
And all the honours that can fly from us
Shall on them settle. You know your places well;
When better fall, for your avails they fell.
Tomorrow to the field.   *Flourish. Exeunt*

SCENE II
The Countess's house.

Enter the Countess and the Clown

COUNTESS   It has happened all as I would have had it,
save that he comes not along with her.

CLOWN   By my faith, I take my young lord to be a very
melancholy man.

COUNTESS   By what observance, I pray you?

CLOWN   Why, he will look upon his boot and sing, mend
the ruff and sing, ask questions and sing, pick his teeth
and sing. I knew a man that had this trick of melancholy
hold a goodly manor for a song.

COUNTESS   Let me see what he writes, and when he
means to come.

She opens the letter

CLOWN   I have no mind to Isbel since I was at Court. Our
old lings and our Isbels of the country are nothing like
your old ling and your Isbels of the Court. The brains of
my Cupid's knocked out, and I begin to love as an old
man loves money, with no stomach.

COUNTESS   What have we here?

CLOWN   Even that you have there.   *Exit*

COUNTESS   (*reading the letter aloud*) *I have sent you a
daughter-in-law; she has recovered the King and undone*

me. I have wedded her, not bedded her, and sworn to
make the 'not' eternal. You shall hear I am run away;
know it before the report comes. If there is breadth
enough in the world I will hold a long distance. My
duty to you.

> Your unfortunate son,
>   Bertram.

This is not well, rash and unbridled boy,
To fly the favours of so good a King,
To pluck his indignation on your head
By the misprizing of a maid too virtuous
For the contempt of empire.

Enter Clown

CLOWN   O madam, yonder is heavy news within, between
two soldiers and my young lady.
COUNTESS   What is the matter?
CLOWN   Nay, there is some comfort in the news, some
comfort: your son will not be killed so soon as I thought
he would.
COUNTESS   Why should he be killed?
CLOWN   So say I, madam, if he runs away, as I hear he
does. The danger is in standing to it; that's the loss of
men, though it is the getting of children. Here they
come will tell you more. For my part, I only hear your
son was run away.   *Exit*

Enter Helena and the two French Lords

FIRST LORD
Save you, good madam.
HELENA
Madam, my lord is gone, for ever gone.

SECOND LORD
    Do not say so.

COUNTESS
    Think upon patience. Pray you, gentlemen—
    I have felt so many quirks of joy and grief
    That the first face of neither on the start
    Can woman me unto it. Where is my son, I pray you?

SECOND LORD
    Madam, he's gone to serve the Duke of Florence.
    We met him thitherward, for thence we came,
    And, after some dispatch in hand at Court,
    Thither we bend again.

HELENA
    Look on his letter, madam: here's my passport.

        (She reads the letter aloud)

When you can get the ring upon my finger, which never
shall come off, and show me a child begotten of your
body that I am father to, then call me husband; but in
such a 'then' I write a 'never'.
    This is a dreadful sentence.

COUNTESS   Brought you this letter, gentlemen?

FIRST LORD   Ay, madam, and for the contents' sake are
    sorry for our pains.

COUNTESS
    I pray you, lady, have a better cheer.
    If you engross all the griefs are yours
    You rob me of a moiety. He was my son,
    But I do wash his name out of my blood
    And you are all my child. Towards Florence is he?

SECOND LORD
    Ay, madam.

COUNTESS   And to be a soldier?

SECOND LORD
 Such is his noble purpose; and, believe it,
 The Duke will lay upon him all the honour
 That good convenience claims.
COUNTESS   Return you thither?
FIRST LORD
 Ay, madam, with the swiftest wing of speed.
HELENA (*reading*)
 Till I have no wife I have nothing in France.
 It is bitter.
COUNTESS Find you that there?
HELENA   Ay, madam.
FIRST LORD It is but the boldness of his hand, haply,
 which his heart was not consenting to.
COUNTESS
 Nothing in France until he has no wife!
 There's nothing here that is too good for him
 But only she; and she deserves a lord
 That twenty such rude boys might tend upon
 And call her, hourly, mistress. Who was with him?
FIRST LORD A servant only, and a gentleman whom I
 have sometime known.
COUNTESS Parolles, was it not?
FIRST LORD Ay, my good lady, he.
COUNTESS
 A very tainted fellow, and full of wickedness.
 My son corrupts a well-derivèd nature
 With his inducement.
FIRST LORD   Indeed, good lady,
 The fellow has a deal of that too much
 Which profits him much to have.
COUNTESS   You are welcome, gentlemen.
 I will entreat you, when you see my son,
 To tell him that his sword can never win
 The honour that he loses. More I'll entreat you
 Written to bear along.

SECOND LORD   We serve you, madam,
    In that and all your worthiest affairs.
COUNTESS
    Not so, but as we change our courtesies.
    Will you draw near? *Exeunt the Countess and the Lords*
HELENA
    'Till I have no wife I have nothing in France.'
    Nothing in France until he has no wife!
    You shall have none, Rossillion, none in France,
    Then have you all again. Poor lord, is it I
    That chase you from your country, and expose
    Those tender limbs of yours to the event
    Of the none-sparing war? And is it I
    That drive you from the sportive Court, where you
    Were shot at with fair eyes, to be the mark
    Of smoky muskets? O you leaden messengers,
    That ride upon the violent speed of fire,
    Fly with false aim, move the recovering air
    That sings with piercing, do not touch my lord.
    Whoever shoots at him, I set him there.
    Whoever charges on his forward breast,
    I am the miscreant that do hold him to it;
    And though I kill him not, I am the cause
    His death was so effected. Better it were
    I met the ravenous lion when he roared
    With sharp constraint of hunger; better it were
    That all the miseries which nature owns
    Were mine at once. No, come you home, Rossillion,
    Whence honour but of danger wins a scar,
    As oft it loses all. I will be gone;
    My being here it is that holds you hence.
    Shall I stay here to do it? No, no, although
    The air of paradise did fan the house
    And angels officed all. I will be gone,
    That pitiful rumour may report my flight

To consolate your ear. Come, night; end, day!
For with the dark, poor thief, I'll steal away.   *Exit*

SCENE III
Florence. Before the Duke's palace.

Flourish. Enter the Duke of Florence, Bertram, Parolles,
soldiers, drum and trumpets

DUKE
    The general of our horse you are, and we,
    Great in our hope, lay our best love and credence
    Upon your promising fortune.
BERTRAM   Sir, it is
    A charge too heavy for my strength; but yet
    We'll strive to bear it for your worthy sake
    To the extreme edge of hazard.
DUKE   Then go you forth,
    And fortune play upon your prosperous helm
    As your auspicious mistress!
BERTRAM   This very day,
    Great Mars, I put myself into your file;
    Make me but like my thoughts and I shall prove
    A lover of your drum, hater of love.   *Exeunt*

SCENE IV
The Countess's house.

Enter the Countess and the Steward

COUNTESS
    Alas! and would you take the letter of her?
    Might you not know she would do as she has done
    By sending me a letter? Read it again.

STEWARD   *(reading)*
  I am Saint Jaquès' pilgrim, thither gone.
    Ambitious love has so in me offended
  That barefoot plod I the cold ground upon,
    With sainted vow my faults to have amended.
  Write, write, that from the bloody course of war
    My dearest master, your dear son, may hie.
  Bless him at home in peace, while I from far
    His name with zealous fervour sanctify.
  His taken labours bid him me forgive;
    I, his despiteful Juno, sent him forth
  From courtly friends, with camping foes to live
    Where death and danger dog the heels of worth.
  He is too good and fair for death and me;
  Whom I myself embrace to set him free.

COUNTESS
  Ah, what sharp stings are in her mildest words!
  Rinaldo, you did never lack advice so much
  As letting her pass so. Had I spoken with her,
  I could have well diverted her intents,
  Which thus she has prevented.

STEWARD   Pardon me, madam.
  If I had given you this at overnight
  She might have been overtaken; yet she writes
  Pursuit would be but vain.

COUNTESS   What angel shall
  Bless this unworthy husband? He cannot thrive,
  Unless her prayers, whom heaven delights to hear
  And loves to grant, reprieve him from the wrath
  Of greatest justice. Write, write, Rinaldo,
  To this unworthy husband of his wife.
  Let every word weigh heavy of her worth
  That he does weigh too light. My greatest grief,
  Though little he does feel it, set down sharply.
  Dispatch the most convenient messenger.

When haply he shall hear that she is gone,
He will return; and hope I may that she,
Hearing so much, will speed her foot again,
Led hither by pure love. Which of them both
Is dearer to me I have no skill in sense
To make distinction. Provide this messenger.
My heart is heavy and my age is weak;
Grief would have tears, and sorrow bids me speak.

Exeunt

SCENE V
Outside the walls of Florence.

*A tucket afar off. Enter Widow of Florence, her
daughter Diana, and Mariana, with citizens*

WIDOW   Nay, come, for if they do approach the city, we
shall lose all the sight.

DIANA   They say the French Count has done most
honourable service.

WIDOW   It is reported that he has taken their greatest
commander, and that with his own hand he slew the
Duke's brother.

Tucket

We have lost our labour; they are gone a contrary way.
Hark! You may know by their trumpets.

MARIANA   Come, let's return again and suffice ourselves
with the report of it. Well, Diana, take heed of this
French Earl. The honour of a maid is her name, and no
legacy is so rich as chastity.

WIDOW   I have told my neighbour how you have been
solicited by a gentleman his companion.

MARIANA   I know that knave, hang him! one Parolles; a
    filthy officer he is in those suggestions for the young
    Earl. Beware of them, Diana: their promises, enticements,
    oaths, tokens, and all these engines of lust, are not the
    things they pass for. Many a maid has been seduced by
    them, and the misery is, example, that so terribly shows
    in the wreck of maidenhood, cannot for all that dissuade
    others, but that they are limed with the twigs that
    threaten them. I hope I need not to advise you further;
    but I hope your own grace will keep you where you are,
    though there is no further danger known but the chastity
    which is so lost.

DIANA   You shall not need to fear me.

Enter Helena

WIDOW   I hope so. Look, here comes a pilgrim. I know
    she will lie at my house; thither they send one another.
    I'll question her. God save you, pilgrim! Whither are
    bound?

HELENA
    To Saint Jaques le Grand.
    Where do the palmers lodge, I do beseech you?

WIDOW
    At the Saint Francis here beside the gate.

HELENA
    Is this the way?

A march afar

WIDOW
    Ay, for sure, it is. Hark you, they come this way.
    If you will tarry, holy pilgrim,
    But till the troops come by,
    I will conduct you where you shall be lodged;

The rather for I think I know your hostess
As ample as myself.

HELENA   Is it yourself?

WIDOW

If you shall please so, pilgrim.

HELENA

I thank you and will stay upon your leisure.

WIDOW

You came, I think, from France?

HELENA   I did so.

WIDOW

Here you shall see a countryman of yours
That has done worthy service.

HELENA   His name, I pray you?

DIANA

The Count Rossillion. Know you such a one?

HELENA

But by the ear, that hears most nobly of him;
His face I know not.

DIANA   Whatsoever he is,
He's bravely taken here. He stole from France,
As it is reported, for the King had married him
Against his liking. Think you it is so?

HELENA

Ay, surely, merely the truth. I know his lady.

DIANA

There is a gentleman that serves the Count
Reports but coarsely of her.

HELENA   What's his name?

DIANA

Monsieur Parolles.

HELENA   O, I believe with him,
In argument of praise or to the worth
Of the great Count himself, she is too mean
To have her name repeated. All her deserving
Is a reservèd chastity, and that
I have not heard examined.

DIANA   Alas, poor lady!
  'Tis a hard bondage to become the wife
  Of a detesting lord.
WIDOW
  I warrant, good creature, wheresoever she is,
  Her heart weighs sadly. This young maid might do her
  A shrewd turn if she pleased.
HELENA   How do you mean?
  Maybe the amorous Count solicits her
  In the unlawful purpose?
WIDOW   He does indeed,
  And bargains with all that can in such a suit
  Corrupt the tender honour of a maid.
  But she is armed for him and keeps her guard
  In chastity's defence.

Drum and colours. Enter Bertram, Parolles, with soldiers

MARIANA   The gods forbid else!
WIDOW
  So, now they come.
  That is Antonio, the Duke's eldest son;
  That Escalus.
HELENA   Which is the Frenchman?
DIANA   He—
  That with the plume. 'Tis a most gallant fellow.
  I would he loved his wife; if he were chaster
  He were much goodlier. Is't not a handsome gentleman?
HELENA
  I like him well.
DIANA
  'Tis pity he is not chaste. Yon's that same knave
  That leads him to these places. Were I his lady
  I would poison that vile rascal.
HELENA   Which is he?

DIANA   That jackanapes with scarfs. Why is he
  melancholy?
HELENA   Perchance he's hurt in the battle.
PAROLLES   Lose our drum! Well!
MARIANA   He's very vexed at something. Look, he has
  spied us.
WIDOW   Indeed, hang you!
MARIANA   And your courtesy, for a ring-carrier!
                  Exeunt Bertram, Parolles, and soldiers
WIDOW
  The troop is past. Come, pilgrim, I will bring you
  Where you shall host. Of enjoined penitents
  There are four or five, to great Saint Jaquès bound,
  Already at my house.
HELENA   I humbly thank you.
  Please it this matron and this gentle maid
  To eat with us tonight; the charge and thanking
  Shall be for me and, to requite you further,
  I will bestow some precepts on this virgin,
  Worthy the note.
WIDOW *and* MARIANA
        We'll take your offer kindly.   *Exeunt*

SCENE VI
Camp before Florence.

Enter Bertram and the two French Lords

FIRST LORD   Nay, good my lord, put him to it, let him
  have his way.
SECOND LORD   If your lordship finds him not a rascal,
  hold me no more in your respect.
FIRST LORD   On my life, my lord, a bubble.
BERTRAM   Do you think I am so far deceived in him?
FIRST LORD   Believe it, my lord, in my own direct

knowledge; without any malice, but to speak of him as
if my kinsman, he's a most notable coward, an infinite
and endless liar, an hourly promise-breaker, the owner of
no one good quality worthy your lordship's entertainment.

SECOND LORD   It were fit you knew him; lest, reposing
too far in his virtue which he has not, he might at some
great and trusty business in a main danger fail you.

BERTRAM   I would I knew in what particular action to
try him.

SECOND LORD   None better than to let him fetch off his
drum, which you hear him so confidently undertake to do.

FIRST LORD   I, with a troop of Florentines, will suddenly
surprise him; such I will have whom I am sure he
knows not from the enemy. We will bind and hoodwink
him so, that he shall suppose no other but that he is
carried into the camp of the adversaries, when we bring
him to our own tents. Be but your lordship present at
his examination. If he does not for the promise of his
life, and in the highest compulsion of base fear, offer to
betray you and deliver all the intelligence in his power
against you, and that with the divine forfeit of his soul
upon oath, never trust my judgement in anything.

SECOND LORD   O, for the love of laughter, let him fetch
his drum; he says he has a stratagem for it. When your
lordship sees the bottom of his success in it, and to what
metal this counterfeit lump of ore will be melted, if you
give him not John Drum's entertainment your inclining
cannot be removed. Here he comes.

Enter Parolles

FIRST LORD   O, for the love of laughter, hinder not the
honour of his design; let him fetch off his drum in any
hand.

BERTRAM   How now, monsieur! This drum sticks sorely
in your disposition.

SECOND LORD   A pox on it! Let it go, it is but a drum.

PAROLLES   But a drum! Is it but a drum? A drum so lost!
There was excellent command: to charge in with our
horse upon our own wings and to rend our own soldiers!

SECOND LORD   That was not to be blamed in the command
of the service; it was a disaster of war that Caesar
himself could not have prevented, if he had been there
to command.

BERTRAM   Well, we cannot greatly condemn our luck;
some dishonour we had in the loss of that drum, but it
is not to be recovered.

PAROLLES   It might have been recovered.

BERTRAM   It might, but it is not now.

PAROLLES   It is to be recovered. But that the merit of service
is seldom attributed to the true and exact performer, I
would have that drum or another, or *hic jacet.* [Here he
lies.]

BERTRAM   Why, if you have a stomach, to it, monsieur!
If you think your mystery in stratagem can bring this
instrument of honour again into its native quarter, be
magnanimous in the enterprise and go on. I will grace
the attempt for a worthy exploit. If you speed well in it
the Duke shall both speak of it and extend to you what
further becomes his greatness, even to the utmost syllable
of your worthiness.

PAROLLES   By the hand of a soldier, I will undertake it.

BERTRAM   But you must not now slumber in it.

PAROLLES   I'll about it this evening, and I will at once pen
down my dilemmas, encourage myself in my certainty,
put myself into my mortal preparation. And by midnight
look to hear further from me.

BERTRAM   May I be bold to acquaint his grace you are
gone about it?

PAROLLES   I know not what the success will be, my lord,
but the attempt I vow.

BERTRAM   I know you are valiant, and to the capability
of your soldiership will subscribe for you. Farewell.

PAROLLES   I love not many words.   *Exit*

FIRST LORD   No more than a fish loves water. Is not this a
strange fellow, my lord, that so confidently seems to
undertake this business; which he knows is not to be
done, damns himself to do, and dares better be damned
than to do it.

SECOND LORD   You do not know him, my lord, as we do.
Certain it is that he will steal himself into a man's
favour and for a week escape a great deal of discoveries;
but when you find him out you know him ever after.

BERTRAM   Why, do you think he will make no deed at
all of this that so seriously he does address himself
unto?

FIRST LORD   None in the world, but return with an
invention, and clap upon you two or three probable
lies. But we have almost run him down. You shall see
his fall tonight; for indeed he is not for your lordship's
respect.

SECOND LORD   We'll make you some sport with the fox
ere we cage him. He was first shown up by the old Lord
Lafew. When his disguise and he are parted tell me
what a sprat you shall find him; which you shall see
this very night.

FIRST LORD   I must go look to my twigs. He shall be
caught.

BERTRAM   Your brother, he shall go along with me.

FIRST LORD   As it pleases your lordship. I'll leave you.

                                                              Exit

BERTRAM

Now will I lead you to the house and show you
The lass I spoke of.

SECOND LORD   But you say she's chaste.

BERTRAM

    That's all the fault. I spoke with her but once
    And found her wondrous cold. But I sent to her
    By this same coxcomb that we have in the wind
    Tokens and letters which she did re-send,
    And this is all I have done. She's a fair creature;
    Will you go see her?

SECOND LORD   With all my heart, my lord.   *Exeunt*

SCENE VII
Florence. The Widow's house.

Enter Helena and the Widow

HELENA

    If you misdoubt me that I am not she,
    I know not how I shall assure you further
    But I shall lose the grounds I work upon.

WIDOW

    Though my estate is fallen, I was well born,
    Nothing acquainted with these businesses,
    And would not put my reputation now
    In any staining act.

HELENA   Nor would I wish you.
    First give me trust the Count he is my husband,
    And what to your sworn counsel I have spoken
    Is so from word to word; and then you cannot,
    By the good aid that I of you shall borrow,
    Err in bestowing it.

WIDOW   I should believe you,
    For you have shown me that which well approves
    You are great in fortune.

HELENA   Take this purse of gold,
    And let me buy your friendly help thus far,
    Which I will over-pay, and pay again

When I have found it. The Count he woos your daughter,
Lays down his wanton siege before her beauty,
Resolved to carry her. Let her, in fine, consent
As we'll direct her how 'tis best to bear it.
Now his importunate blood will naught deny
That she'll demand. A ring the Count does wear
That downward has succeeded in his house
From son to son some four or five descents
Since the first father wore it. This ring he holds
In most rich choice; yet, in his idle fire,
To buy his will it would not seem too dear,
However repented after.

WIDOW   Now I see
The bottom of your purpose.

HELENA
You see it lawful then. It is no more
But that your daughter, ere she seems as won,
Desires this ring; appoints him an encounter;
In short, delivers me to fill the time,
Herself most chastely absent. After,
To marry her I'll add three thousand crowns
To what is passed already.

WIDOW   I have yielded.
Instruct my daughter how she shall persèver.
That time and place with this deceit so lawful
May prove coherent. Every night he comes
With music of all sorts, and songs composed
To her unworthiness. It nothing helps us
To chide him from our eaves, for he persists
As if his life lay on it.

HELENA   Why then tonight
Let us assay our plot, which, if it speed,
Is wicked meaning in a lawful deed,
And lawful meaning in a lawful act,
Where both not sin, and yet a sinful fact.
But let us about it.   *Exeunt*

Act IV

❀

SCENE I
Outside the Florentine camp.

Enter the First French Lord, with Soldiers in ambush

FIRST LORD   He can come no other way but by this hedgecorner. When you sally upon him speak what terrible language you will; though you understand it not yourselves, no matter; for we must not seem to understand him, unless some one among us, whom we must produce for an interpreter.

FIRST SOLDIER   Good captain, let me be the interpreter.

FIRST LORD   Are you not acquainted with him? Knows he not your voice?

FIRST SOLDIER   No, sir, I warrant you.

FIRST LORD   But what mish-mash have you to speak to us again?

FIRST SOLDIER   Even such as you speak to me.

FIRST LORD   He must think us some band of foreigners in the adversary's entertainment. Now he has a smack of all neighbouring languages, therefore we must every one be a man of his own fancy, not to know what we speak one to another; so we seem to know is to know straight our purpose—choughs' language, gabble enough and good enough. As for you, interpreter, you must seem very politic. But couch, ho! Here he comes to beguile two hours in a sleep, and then to return and swear the lies he forges.

Enter Parolles

83

PAROLLES   Ten o'clock. Within these three hours it will
    be time enough to go home. What shall I say I have
    done? It must be a very plausible invention that carries
    it. They begin to suspect me, and disgraces have of late
    knocked too often at my door. I find my tongue is too
    foolhardy, but my heart has the fear of Mars before it
    and of his creatures, not daring the reports of my tongue.
FIRST LORD   This is the first truth that ever your own
    tongue was guilty of.
PAROLLES   What the devil should move me to undertake
    the recovery of this drum, being not ignorant of the
    impossibility, and knowing I had no such purpose? I
    must give myself some hurts, and say I got them in an
    exploit. Yet slight ones will not carry it: they will say
    'Came you off with so little?' And great ones I dare not
    give. Wherefore, what's the instance? Tongue, I must
    put you into a butter-woman's mouth, and buy myself
    another of Bajazeth's mule, if you prattle me into these
    perils.
FIRST LORD   Is it possible he should know what he is,
    and be that he is?
PAROLLES   I would the cutting of my garments would
    serve the turn, or the breaking of my Spanish sword.
FIRST LORD   We cannot afford you so.
PAROLLES   Or the baring of my beard, and to say it was in
    stratagem.
FIRST LORD   It would not do.
PAROLLES   Or to drown my clothes and say I was stripped.
FIRST LORD   Hardly serve.
PAROLLES   Though I swore I leaped from the window of
    the citadel—
FIRST LORD   How deep?
PAROLLES   Thirty fathom.
FIRST LORD   Three great oaths would scarce make that be
    believed.

PAROLLES   I would I had any drum of the enemy's; I
    would swear I recovered it.
FIRST LORD   You shall hear one anon.
PAROLLES   A drum now of the enemy's—

Alarum within

FIRST LORD   *Throca movousus, cargo, cargo, cargo.*
ALL   *Cargo, cargo, cargo, villianda par corbo, cargo.*

They seize him

PAROLLES
    O, ransom, ransom!

They blindfold him

                    Do not hide my eyes.
FIRST SOLDIER   *Boskos thromuldo boskos.*
PAROLLES
    I know you are the Muskos' regiment,
    And I shall lose my life for want of language.
    If there be here German, or Dane, Low Dutch,
    Italian, or French, let him speak to me,
    I'll discover that which shall undo the Florentine.
FIRST SOLDIER   *Boskos vauvado.* I understand you, and
    can speak your tongue. *Kerelybonto.* Sir, betake you to
    your faith, for seventeen poniards are at your bosom.
PAROLLES   O!
FIRST SOLDIER   O, pray, pray, pray! *Manka revania dulche.*
FIRST LORD   *Oscorbidulchos volivorco.*
FIRST SOLDIER
    The General is content to spare you yet,
    And, blindfold as you are, will lead you on
    To gather from you. Haply you may inform
    Something to save your life.

PAROLLES   O, let me live,
    And all the secrets of our camp I'll show,
    Their force, their purposes; nay, I'll speak that
    Which you will wonder at.
FIRST SOLDIER   But will you faithfully?
PAROLLES
    If I do not, damn me.
FIRST SOLDIER   *Acordo linta.*
    Come on, you are granted space.
                                Exit with Parolles guarded

                    A short alarum within

FIRST LORD
    Go tell the Count Rossillion and my brother
    We have caught the woodcock and will keep him muffled
    Till we do hear from them.
SECOND SOLDIER   Captain, I will.
FIRST LORD
    He will betray us all unto ourselves:
    Inform on that.
SECOND SOLDIER
    So I will, sir.
FIRST LORD
    Till then I'll keep him dark and safely locked.   *Exeunt*

                    SCENE II
                The Widow's house.

                Enter Bertram and Diana

BERTRAM
    They told me that your name was Fontibell.

DIANA
  No, my good lord, Diana.
BERTRAM   Titled goddess,
  And worth it, with addition! But, fair soul,
  In your fine frame has love no quality?
  If the quick fire of youth light not your mind
  You are no maiden but a monument.
  When you are dead you should be such a one
  As you are now; for you are cold and stern,
  And now you should be as your mother was
  When your sweet self was got.
DIANA
  She then was chaste.
BERTRAM   So should you be.
DIANA   No.
  My mother did but duty—such, my lord,
  As you owe to your wife.
BERTRAM   No more of that!
  I pray you do not strive against my vows.
  I was compelled to her, but I love you
  By love's own sweet constraint, and will for ever
  Do you all rights of service.
DIANA   Ay, so you serve us
  Till we serve you; but when you have our roses,
  You barely leave our thorns to prick ourselves,
  And mock us with our bareness.
BERTRAM   How have I sworn!
DIANA
  It is not the many oaths that make the truth,
  But the plain single vow that is vowed true.
  What is not holy, that we swear not by,
  But take the highest to witness. Then, pray you, tell me:
  If I should swear by Love's great attributes
  I loved you dearly, would you believe my oaths
  When I did love you ill? This has no holding,
  To swear by him whom I protest to love

That I will work against him. Therefore your oaths
Are words, and poor conditions but unsealed—
At least in my opinion.

BERTRAM   Change it, change it.
Be not so holy-cruel. Love is holy,
And my integrity never knew the crafts
That you do charge men with. Stand no more off,
But give yourself unto my sick desires,
Who then recovers. Say you are mine, and ever
My love as it begins shall so persèver.

DIANA
I see that men make vows in such a flame
That we'll forsake ourselves. Give me that ring.

BERTRAM
I'll lend it you, my dear, but have no power
To give it from me.

DIANA   Will you not, my lord?

BERTRAM
It is an honour belonging to our house,
Bequeathèd down from many ancestors,
Which were the greatest obloquy in the world
In me to lose.

DIANA   My honour is such a ring;
My chastity's the jewel of our house,
Bequeathèd down from many ancestors,
Which were the greatest obloquy in the world
In me to lose. Thus your own self's wisdom
Brings in the champion Honour on my part
Against your vain assault.

BERTRAM   Here, take my ring.
My house, my honour, yea, my life be yours,
And I'll be bidden by you.

DIANA
When midnight comes, knock at my chamber window;
I'll order take my mother shall not hear.
Now will I charge you in the band of truth,

When you have conquered my yet maiden bed,
Remain there but an hour, nor speak to me.
My reasons are most strong and you shall know them
When back again this ring shall be delivered.
And on your finger in the night I'll put
Another ring, that what in time proceeds
May token to the future our past deeds.
Adieu till then; then, fail not. You have won
A wife of me, though there my hope is done.

BERTRAM
A heaven on earth I have won by wooing thee.   *Exit*

DIANA
For which live long to thank both heaven and me!
You may so in the end.
My mother told me just how he would woo
As if she sat in his heart. She says all men
Have the like oaths. He had sworn to marry me
When his wife's dead; therefore I'll lie with him
When I am buried. Since Frenchmen are so braid [false].
Marry that will, I live and die a maid.
Only, in this disguise, I think it no sin
To cozen him that would unjustly win.   *Exit*

SCENE III
The Florentine camp.

Enter the two French Lords, and soldiers

FIRST LORD   You have not given him his mother's letter?
SECOND LORD   I have delivered it an hour since. There is
    something in it that stings his nature, for on reading it
    he changed almost into another man.
FIRST LORD   He has much worthy blame laid upon him
    for shaking off so good a wife and so sweet a lady.

SECOND LORD   Especially he has incurred the everlasting
    displeasure of the King, who had even tuned his bounty
    to sing happiness to him. I will tell you a thing, but you
    shall let it dwell darkly with you.

FIRST LORD   When you have spoken it 'tis dead, and I am
    the grave of it.

SECOND LORD   He has perverted a young gentlewoman
    here in Florence, of a most chaste renown, and this
    night he fleshes his will in the spoil of her honour. He
    has given her his monumental ring, and thinks himself
    made in the unchaste composition.

FIRST LORD   Now, God lay our rebellious flesh! As we are
    ourselves, what things are we!

SECOND LORD   Merely our own traitors. And as in the
    common course of all treasons we ever see them reveal
    themselves till they attain to their abhorred ends, so he
    that in this action contrives against his own nobility, in
    his proper stream overflows himself.

FIRST LORD   Is it not meant damnable in us to be trumpeters
    of our unlawful intents? We shall not then have his
    company tonight?

SECOND LORD   Not till after midnight, for he is dieted to
    his hour.

FIRST LORD   That approaches apace. I would gladly have
    him see his company analysed, that he might take a
    measure of his own judgements wherein so curiously he
    had set this counterfeit.

SECOND LORD   We will not meddle with him till he
    comes, for his presence must be the whip of the other.

FIRST LORD   In the meantime, what hear you of these
    wars?

SECOND LORD   I hear there is an overture of peace.

FIRST LORD   Nay, I assure you, a peace concluded.

SECOND LORD   What will Count Rossillion do then?
    Will he travel further, or return again into France?

FIRST LORD   I perceive by this demand you are not
    altogether of his counsel.

SECOND LORD   Let it be forbidden, sir; so should I be a
   great deal of his act.
FIRST LORD   Sir, his wife some two months since fled
   from his house. Her pretence is a pilgrimage to Saint
   Jaques le Grand; which holy undertaking with most
   austere sanctimony she accomplished; and there residing,
   the tenderness of her nature became as a prey to her
   grief; in fine, made a groan of her last breath, and now
   she sings in heaven.
SECOND LORD   How is this borne out?
FIRST LORD   The stronger part of it by her own letters,
   which make her story true even to the point of her
   death. Her death itself, which could not be her office to
   say is come, was faithfully confirmed by the rector of
   the place.
SECOND LORD   Has the Count all this intelligence?
FIRST LORD   Ay, and the particular confirmations, point
   from point, to the full arming of the verity.
SECOND LORD   I am heartily sorry that he'll be glad of
   this.
FIRST LORD   How mightily sometimes we make comforts
   of our losses!
SECOND LORD   And how mightily some other times we
   drown our gain in tears! The great dignity that his
   valour has here acquired for him shall at home be
   encountered with a shame as ample.
FIRST LORD   The web of our life is of a mingled yarn,
   good and ill together. Our virtues would be proud if our
   faults whipped them not, and our crimes would despair
   if they were not cherished by our virtues.

Enter a Messenger

How now? Where's your master?
MESSENGER   He met the Duke in the street, sir, of whom
   he has taken a solemn leave: his lordship will next

morning for France. The Duke has offered him letters of
commendations to the King.

SECOND LORD   They shall be no more than needful there,
if they were more than they can commend.

Enter Bertram

FIRST LORD   They cannot be too sweet for the King's
tartness. Here's his lordship now. How now, my lord? Is
it not after midnight?

BERTRAM   I have tonight dispatched sixteen businesses a
month's length apiece. By an abstract of success: I have
congied with the Duke, done my adieu with his nearest,
buried a wife, mourned for her, writ to my lady mother
I am returning, entertained my convoy, and between
these main parcels of dispatch effected many nicer needs;
the last was the greatest, but that I have not ended yet.

SECOND LORD   If the business is of any difficulty, and
this morning your departure hence, it requires haste of
your lordship.

BERTRAM   I mean, the business is not ended, as fearing
to hear of it hereafter. But shall we have this dialogue
between the Fool and the Soldier? Come, bring forth
this counterfeit image who has deceived me like a
doublemeaning prophesier.

SECOND LORD   Bring him forth.   *Exeunt the Soldiers*
Has sat in the stocks all night, poor gallant knave.

BERTRAM   No matter. His heels have deserved it in
usurping his spurs so long. How does he carry himself?

SECOND LORD   I have told your lordship already: the
stocks carry him. But to answer you as you would be
understood, he weeps like a wench that had spilt her
milk. He has confessed himself to Morgan, whom he
supposes to be a friar, from the time of his remembrance
to this very instant disaster of his setting in the stocks.
And what think you he has confessed?

BERTRAM   Nothing of me, has he?

SECOND LORD   His confession is taken, and it shall be read to his face; if your lordship is in it, as I believe you are, you must have the patience to hear it.

Enter Parolles muffled

BERTRAM   A plague upon him! Muffled! He can say nothing of me.

FIRST LORD   *(aside to Bertram)* Hush, hush! Blindman comes. *(Aloud)* Portotartarossa.

FIRST SOLDIER   He calls for the tortures. What will you say without them?

PAROLLES   I will confess what I know without constraint. If you pinch me like a pasty I can say no more.

FIRST SOLDIER   *Bosko chimurcho.*

FIRST LORD   *Boblibindo chicurmurco.*

FIRST SOLDIER   You are a merciful general. Our General bids you answer to what I shall ask you out of a note.

PAROLLES   And truly, as I hope to live.

FIRST SOLDIER   *(reading)* *First demand of him how many horse the Duke is strong.* What say you to that?

PAROLLES   Five or six thousand, but very weak and unserviceable. The troops are all scattered and the commanders very poor rogues, upon my reputation and credit, and as I hope to live.

FIRST SOLDIER   Shall I set down your answer so?

PAROLLES   Do. I'll take the sacrament on it, how and which way you will.

BERTRAM   All's one to him. What a past-saving slave is this!

FIRST LORD   You are deceived, my lord; this is Monsieur Parolles, the gallant militarist—that was his own phrase—that had the whole theory of war in the knot of his scarf, and the practice in the scabbard of his dagger.

SECOND LORD   I will never trust a man again for keeping
  his sword clean, nor believe he can have everything in
  him by wearing his apparel neatly.

FIRST SOLDIER   Well, that's set down.

PAROLLES   'Five or six thousand horse' I said—I will say
  true—'or thereabouts' set down, for I'll speak truth.

FIRST LORD   He's very near the truth in this.

BERTRAM   But I give him no thanks for it, in the nature
  he delivers it.

PAROLLES   'Poor rogues' I pray you say.

FIRST SOLDIER   Well, that's set down.

PAROLLES   I humbly thank you, sir. A truth's a truth, the
  rogues are marvellous poor.

FIRST SOLDIER   (reading) Demand of him of what strength
  they are a-foot. What say you to that?

PAROLLES   By my faith, sir, if I were to live this present
  hour, I will tell true. Let me see: Spurio, a hundred
  and fifty; Sebastian, so many; Corambus, so many;
  Jaques, so many; Guiltian, Cosmo, Lodowick, and Gratii,
  two hundred fifty each; my own company, Chitopher,
  Vaumond, Bentii, two hundred fifty each. So that the
  muster-file, rotten and sound, upon my life, amounts
  not to fifteen thousand poll; half of which dare not
  shake the snow from off their cassocks lest they shake
  themselves to pieces.

BERTRAM   What shall be done to him?

FIRST LORD   Nothing but let him have thanks. Demand
  of him my condition, and what credit I have with the
  Duke.

FIRST SOLDIER   Well, that's set down. (Reading) You shall
  demand of him whether one Captain Dumaine is in the
  camp, a Frenchman; what his reputation is with the
  Duke, what his valour, honesty, and expertness in wars;
  or whether he thinks it not possible with well-weighing
  sums of gold to corrupt him to a revolt. What say you to
  this? What do you know of it?

PAROLLES   I beseech you, let me answer to the particular
of the interogatories. Demand them singly.

FIRST SOLDIER   Do you know this Captain Dumaine?

PAROLLES   I know him: he was a patcher's prentice in
Paris, from whence he was whipped for getting the
sheriff's fool with child, a dumb innocent that could
not say him nay.

BERTRAM   Nay, by your leave, hold your hands—though
I know his brains are forfeit to the next tile that falls.

FIRST SOLDIER   Well, is this captain in the Duke of
Florence's camp?

PAROLLES   Upon my knowledge he is, and lousy.

FIRST LORD   Nay, look not so upon me; we shall hear of
your lordship anon.

FIRST SOLDIER   What is his reputation with the Duke?

PAROLLES   The Duke knows him for no other but a poor
officer of mine, and wrote to me this other day to turn
him out of the band. I think I have his letter in my
pocket.

FIRST SOLDIER   Sure, we'll search.

PAROLLES   Seriously, I do not know; either it is there or it
is upon a file with the Duke's other letters in my tent.

FIRST SOLDIER   Here it is; here's a paper. Shall I read it to
you?

PAROLLES   I do not know if it is it or no.

BERTRAM   Our interpreter does it well.

FIRST LORD   Excellently.

FIRST SOLDIER   *(reading)*
Dian, the Count's a fool, and full of gold.

PAROLLES   That is not the Duke's letter, sir; that is an
advertisement to a respectable maid in Florence, one
Diana, to take heed of the allurement of one Count
Rossillion, a foolish idle boy, but for all that very ruttish.
I pray you, sir, put it up again.

FIRST SOLDIER   Nay, I'll read it first by your favour.

PAROLLES   My meaning in it, I protest, was very honest
    in the behalf of the maid; for I knew the young Count to
    be a dangerous and lascivious boy, who is a whale to
    virginity, and devours up all the fry it finds.

BERTRAM   Damnable both-sides rogue!

FIRST SOLDIER   (*reading*)

> When he swears oaths, bid him drop gold, and
>   take it;
> After he scores he never pays the score.
> Half-won is match well made; match, and well
>   make it.
> He never pays after-debts, take it before.
> And say a soldier, Dian, told you this:
> Men are to meddle with, boys are not to kiss;
> For count of this, the Count's a fool, I know it,
> Who pays before, but not when he does owe it.
>   Yours, as he vowed to you in your ear,
>   Parolles.

BERTRAM   He shall be whipped through the army, with
    this rhyme in his forehead.

SECOND LORD   This is your devoted friend, sir, the
    manifold linguist, and the armipotent soldier.

BERTRAM   I could endure anything before but a cat, and
    now he's a cat to me.

FIRST SOLDIER   I perceive, sir, by the General's looks, we
    shall be forced to hang you.

PAROLLES   My life, sir, in any case! Not that I am afraid
    to die, but that, my offences being many, I would repent
    out the remainder of nature. Let me live, sir, in a
    dungeon, in the stocks, or anywhere, so I may live.

FIRST SOLDIER   We'll see what may be done, so you confess
    freely. Therefore once more to this Captain Dumaine:
    you have answered to his reputation with the Duke and
    to his valour; what is his honesty?

PAROLLES   He will steal, sir, an egg out of a cloister. For
  rapes and ravishments he parallels Nessus. He professes
  not keeping of oaths; in breaking them he is stronger
  than Hercules. He will lie, sir, with such volubility that
  you would think truth were a fool. Drunkenness is his
  best virtue, for he will be swine-drunk, and in his sleep
  he does little harm, save to his bedclothes about him;
  but they know his conditions and lay him in straw. I
  have but little more to say, sir, of his honesty: he has
  everything that an honest man should not have; what
  an honest man should have, he has nothing.
FIRST LORD   I begin to love him for this.
BERTRAM   For this description of your honesty? A pox
  upon him! For me, he's more and more a cat.
FIRST SOLDIER   What say you to his expertness in war?
PAROLLES   Faith, sir, he has led the drum before the
  English tragedians—to belie him I will not—and more
  of his soldiership I know not, except in that country he
  had the honour to be the officer at a place there called
  Mile-end, to instruct for the doubling of files. I would do
  the man what honour I can, but of this I am not certain.
FIRST LORD   He has out-villained villainy so far that the
  rarity redeems him.
BERTRAM   A pox on him! He's a cat still.
FIRST SOLDIER   His qualities being at this poor price, I
  need not to ask you if gold will corrupt him to revolt.
PAROLLES   Sir, for a quarter he will sell the fee-simple of
  his salvation, the inheritance of it, and cut the entail
  from all remainders, and a perpetual succession for it
  perpetually.
FIRST SOLDIER   What's his brother, the other Captain
  Dumaine?
SECOND LORD   Why does he ask him of me?
FIRST SOLDIER   What is he?
PAROLLES   Even a crow of the same nest; not altogether so
  great as the first in goodness, but greater a great deal in

evil. He excels his brother for a coward, yet his brother
is reputed one of the best that is. In a retreat he outruns
any lackey; however, in coming on he has the cramp.

FIRST SOLDIER   If your life is saved will you undertake to
betray the Florentine?

PAROLLES   Ay, and the captain of his horse, Count
Rossillion.

FIRST SOLDIER   I'll whisper with the General and know
his pleasure.

PAROLLES   I'll no more drumming. A plague of all
drums! Only to seem to deserve well, and to beguile the
supposition of that lascivious young boy, the Count,
have I run into this danger. Yet who would have suspected
an ambush where I was taken?

FIRST SOLDIER   There is no remedy, sir, but you must die.
The General says you that have so traitorously discovered
the secrets of your army, and made such pestiferous
reports of men very nobly held, can serve the world for
no honest use; therefore you must die. Come, headsman,
off with his head.

PAROLLES   O Lord, sir, let me live, or let me see my
death!

FIRST SOLDIER   That shall you, and take your leave of all
your friends.

He unmuffles him

So: look about you. Know you any here?

BERTRAM   Good morrow, noble captain.

SECOND LORD   God bless you, Captain Parolles.

FIRST LORD   God save you, noble captain.

SECOND LORD   Captain, what greeting will you to my
Lord Lafew? I am for France.

FIRST LORD   Good captain, will you give me a copy
of the sonnet you writ to Diana in behalf of the Count

Rossillion? If I were not a very coward I'd compel it of
you; but fare you well.

Exeunt Bertram and the Lords

FIRST SOLDIER   You are undone, captain—all but your
scarf; that has a knot in it yet.

PAROLLES   Who cannot be crushed with a plot?

FIRST SOLDIER   If you could find out a country where but
women were that had received so much shame, you
might begin an impudent nation. Fare you well, sir. I
am for France too; we shall speak of you there.

Exeunt the Soldiers

PAROLLES

Yet am I thankful. If my heart were great
It would burst at this. Captain I'll be no more,
But I will eat and drink and sleep as soft
As captain shall. Simply the thing I am
Shall make me live. Who knows himself a braggart,
Let him fear this; for it will come to pass
That every braggart shall be found an ass.
Rust, sword; cool, blushes; and Parolles live
Safest in shame; being fooled, by foolery thrive.
There's place and means for every man alive.
I'll after them.   *Exit*

SCENE IV
The Widow's house.

Enter Helena, the Widow, and Diana

HELENA

That you may well perceive I have not wronged you
One of the greatest in the Christian world
Shall be my surety; before whose throne 'tis needful,
Ere I can perfect my intents, to kneel.
Time was, I did him a desirèd office,

Dear almost as his life, which gratitude
Through flinty Tartar's bosom would peep forth
And answer thanks. I duly am informed
His grace is at Marseillès, to which place
We have convenient convoy. You must know
I am supposèd dead. The army breaking,
My husband hies him home where, heaven aiding,
And by the leave of my good lord the King,
We'll be before our welcome.

WIDOW   Gentle madam,
You never had a servant to whose trust
Your business was more welcome.

HELENA   Nor you, mistress,
Ever a friend whose thoughts more truly labour
To recompense your love. Doubt not but heaven
Has brought me up to be your daughter's dower,
As it has fated her to be my motive
And helper to a husband. But, O strange men!
That can such sweet use make of what they hate,
When saucy trusting of the cozened thoughts
Defiles the pitchy night. So lust does play
With what it loathes for that which is away.
But more of this hereafter. You, Diana,
Under my poor instructions yet must suffer
Something in my behalf.

DIANA   Let death and honesty
Go with your impositions, I am yours,
Upon your will to suffer.

HELENA   Yet, I pray you.
But with the word the time will bring on summer,
When briars shall have leaves as well as thorns
And be as sweet as sharp. We must away;
Our wagon is prepared, and time revives us.
All's well that ends well; ever the fine's the crown.
Whatever the course, the end is the renown.   *Exeunt*

SCENE V
The Countess's house.

Enter the Countess, Lafew, and the Clown

LAFEW   No, no, no, your son was misled with a snipped
taffeta fellow there, whose villainous saffron would
have made all the unbaked and doughy youth of a
nation in his colour. Your daughter-in-law had been
alive at this hour, and your son here at home, more
advanced by the King than by that red-tailed bumble-
bee I speak of.

COUNTESS   I would I had not known him; it was the
death of the most virtuous gentlewoman that ever nature
had praise for creating. If she had partaken of my flesh
and cost me the dearest groans of a mother I could not
have owed her a more rooted love.

LAFEW   'Twas a good lady, 'twas a good lady. We may
pick a thousand salads ere we light on such another
herb.

CLOWN   Indeed, sir, she was the sweet-marjoram of the
salad, or, rather, the herb rue.

LAFEW   They are not herbs, you knave, they are scented
herbs.

CLOWN   I am no great Nebuchadnezzar, sir, I have not
much skill in grass.

LAFEW   Which do you profess yourself, a knave or a fool?

CLOWN   A fool, sir, at a woman's service, and a knave at
a man's.

LAFEW   Your distinction?

CLOWN   I would cozen the man of his wife and do his
service.

LAFEW   So you were a knave at his service indeed.

CLOWN   And I would give his wife my bauble, sir, to do
her service.

LAFEW   I will subscribe for you, you are both knave and
fool.

CLOWN   At your service.

LAFEW   No, no, no.

CLOWN   Why, sir, if I cannot serve you I can serve as
great a prince as you are.

LAFEW   Who's that? A Frenchman?

CLOWN   Faith, sir, he has an English name; but his
physiognomy is hotter in France than there.

LAFEW   What prince is that?

CLOWN   The Black Prince, sir, alias the prince of darkness,
alias the devil.

LAFEW   Hold, there's my purse. I give you not this to
tempt you from your master you talk of; serve him still.

CLOWN   I am a woodland fellow, sir, that always loved a
great fire, and the master I speak of ever keeps a good
fire. But sure he is the prince of the world; let his
nobility remain in his Court. I am for the house with
the narrow gate, which I take to be too little for pomp to
enter; some that humble themselves may, but the many
will be too chill and tender, and they'll be for the
flowery way that leads to the broad gate and the great
fire.

LAFEW   Go your ways. I begin to be aweary of you, and I
tell you so before, because I would not fall out with you.
Go your ways. Let my horses be well looked to, without
any tricks.

CLOWN   If I put any tricks upon them, sir, they shall be
jades' tricks, which are their own right by the law of
nature.   *Exit*

LAFEW   A shrewd knave and an unhappy.

COUNTESS   So he is. My lord that's gone made himself
much sport out of him; by his authority he remains
here, which he thinks is a patent for his sauciness; and
indeed he has no pace, but runs where he will.

LAFEW   I like him well, 'tis not amiss. And I was about
   to tell you, since I heard of the good lady's death
   and that my lord your son was upon his return home, I
   moved the King my master to speak in the behalf of my
   daughter; which, in the minority of them both, his
   majesty out of a self-gracious remembrance did first
   propose. His highness has promised me to do it; and to
   stop up the displeasure he has conceived against your
   son there is no fitter matter. How does your ladyship
   like it?

COUNTESS   With very much content, my lord, and I
   wish it happily effected.

LAFEW   His highness comes post from Marseilles, of
   as able body as when he numbered thirty. He will
   be here tomorrow, or I am deceived by him that in such
   intelligence has seldom failed.

COUNTESS   It rejoices me that I hope I shall see him ere I
   die. I have letters that my son will be here tonight. I
   shall beseech your lordship to remain with me till they
   meet together.

LAFEW   Madam, I was thinking with what manners I
   might safely be admitted.

COUNTESS   You need but plead your honourable privilege.

LAFEW   Lady, of that I have made a bold charter but, I
   thank my God, it holds yet.

Enter Clown

CLOWN   O madam, yonder's my lord your son with a
   patch of velvet on his face; whether there is a scar under
   it or no, the velvet knows, but it is a goodly patch of
   velvet. His left cheek is a cheek of two pile and a half,
   but his right cheek is worn bare.

LAFEW   A scar nobly got, or a noble scar, is a good livery
   of honour; so likely is that.

CLOWN   But it is your ulcerated face.

LAFEW   Let us go see your son, I pray you. I long to talk
    with the young noble soldier.

CLOWN   Faith, there's a dozen of them with delicate fine
    hats, and most courteous feathers which bow the head
    and nod at every man.   *Exeunt*

Act V

SCENE I
Marseilles. A street.

Enter Helena, the Widow, and Diana, with two attendants

HELENA

But this exceeding posting day and night
Must wear your spirits low. We cannot help it;
But since you have made the days and nights as one
To wear your gentle limbs in my affairs,
Be bold you do so grow in my requital
As nothing can unroot you.

Enter a Gentleman to the King

In happy time!
This man may help me to his majesty's ear,
If he would spend his power. God save you, sir!

GENTLEMAN

And you.

HELENA

Sir, I have seen you in the court of France.

GENTLEMAN

I have been sometimes there.

HELENA

I do presume, sir, that you are not fallen
From the report that goes upon your goodness;
And therefore, goaded with most sharp occasions
Which lay nice manners by, I put you to
The use of your own virtues, for ever which

I shall continue thankful.

GENTLEMAN   What is your will?

HELENA

That it will please you
To give this poor petition to the King,
And aid me with that store of power you have
To come into his presence.

GENTLEMAN

The King is not here.

HELENA   Not here, sir?

GENTLEMAN   Not indeed.

He hence removed last night, and with more haste
Than is his use.

WIDOW   Lord, how we lose our pains!

HELENA

All's well that ends well yet,
Though time seems so adverse and means unfit.
I do beseech you, whither is he gone?

GENTLEMAN

Indeed, as I take it, to Rossillion;
Whither I am going.

HELENA   I do beseech you, sir,
Since you are likely to see the King before me,
Commend the paper to his gracious hand,
Which I presume shall render you no blame,
But rather make you thank your pains for it.
I will come after you with what good speed
Our means will make us means.

GENTLEMAN   This I'll do for you.

HELENA

And you shall find yourself to be well thanked,
Whatever falls more. We must to horse again.
Go, go, provide.   *Exeunt*

SCENE II
Before the Countess's house.

Enter the Clown and Parolles

PAROLLES Good Master Lavatch, give my Lord Lafew
this letter. I have ere now, sir, been better known to you,
when I have held familiarity with fresher clothes; but I
am now, sir, muddied in Fortune's mood, and smell
somewhat strong of her strong displeasure.

CLOWN Truly, Fortune's displeasure is but sluttish if it
smells so strongly as you speak of. I will henceforth eat
no fish of Fortune's buttering. Pray, allow me the wind.

PAROLLES Nay, you need not to stop your nose, sir. I
spoke but by a metaphor.

CLOWN Indeed, sir, if your metaphor stinks I will stop
my nose, or against any man's metaphor. Pray, get you
further.

PAROLLES Pray you, sir, deliver me this paper.

CLOWN Foh! Pray stand away. A paper from Fortune's
close-stool, to give to a nobleman! Look, here he comes
himself.

Enter Lafew

Here is a purr of Fortune's sir, or of Fortune's cat, but not
a musk-cat, that has fallen into the unclean fishpond
of her displeasure and, as he says, is muddied with it.
Pray you, sir, use the carp as you may, for he looks
like a poor, decayed, ingenious, foolish, rascally knave.
I do pity his distress in my similes of comfort, and
leave him to your lordship.   *Exit*

PAROLLES My lord, I am a man whom Fortune has cruelly
scratched.

LAFEW And what would you have me to do? It is too late

to pare her nails now. Wherein have you played the knave with Fortune that she should scratch you, who of herself is a good lady and would not have knaves thrive long under her? There's a quarter for you. Let the justices make you and Fortune friends; I am for other business.

PAROLLES   I beseech your honour to hear me one single word.

LAFEW   You beg a single penny more. Come, you shall have it, save your word.

PAROLLES   My name, my good lord, is Parolles.

LAFEW   You beg more than 'word' then. God's passion! Give me your hand. How does your drum?

PAROLLES   O my good lord, you were the first that found me.

LAFEW   Was I, in truth? And I was the first that lost you.

PAROLLES   It lies in you, my lord, to bring me in some grace, for you did bring me out.

LAFEW   Out upon you, knave! Do you put upon me at once both the office of God and the devil? One brings you in grace and the other brings you out.

Trumpets sound

The King's coming; I know by his trumpets. Fellow, inquire further after me. I had talk of you last night. Though you are a fool and a knave you shall eat. Get on, follow.

PAROLLES   I praise God for you.   *Exeunt*

SCENE III
The Countess's house.

Flourish. Enter the King, the Countess, Lafew, the two French Lords, with attendants

KING
    We lost a jewel of her, and our esteem
    Was made much poorer by it; but your son,
    As mad in folly, lacked the sense to know
    Her estimation home.
COUNTESS   It is past, my liege,
    And I beseech your majesty to make it
    Natural rebellion done in the blade of youth,
    When oil and fire, too strong for reason's force,
    Overbear it and burn on.
KING   My honoured lady,
    I have forgiven and forgotten all,
    Though my revenges were high bent upon him
    And watched the time to shoot.
LAFEW   This I must say—
    But first I beg my pardon—the young lord
    Did to his majesty, his mother, and his lady
    Offence of mighty note, but to himself
    The greatest wrong of all. He lost a wife
    Whose beauty did astonish the survey
    Of richest eyes, whose words all ears took captive,
    Whose dear perfection hearts that scorned to serve
    Humbly called mistress.
KING   Praising what is lost
    Makes the remembrance dear. Well, call him hither;
    We are reconciled, and the first view shall kill
    All repetition. Let him not ask your pardon;
    The nature of his great offence is dead,
    And deeper than oblivion we do bury
    The incensing relics of it. Let him approach
    A stranger, no offender; and inform him
    So it is our will he should.
ATTENDANT   I shall, my liege.   *Exit*

KING

    What says he to your daughter? Have you spoken?

LAFEW

    All that he is has reference to your highness.

KING

    Then shall we have a match. I have letters sent me
    That sets him high in fame.

Enter Bertram

LAFEW   He looks well on it.

KING

    I am not a day of season,
    For you may see a sunshine and a hail
    In me at once. But to the brightest beams
    Distracted clouds give way; so stand you forth:
    The time is fair again.

BERTRAM   My high-repented blames,
    Dear sovereign, pardon to me.

KING   All is whole.

    Not one word more of the consumèd time.
    Let's take the instant by the forward top;
    For we are old, and on our quickest decrees
    The inaudible and noiseless foot of time
    Steals ere we can effect them. You remember
    The daughter of this lord?

BERTRAM

    Admiringly, my liege. At first
    I stuck my choice upon her, ere my heart
    Durst make too bold a herald of my tongue;
    Where, the impression of my eye infixing,
    Contempt his scornful perspective did lend me,
    Which warped the line of every other favour,
    Scorned a fair colour or expressed it stolen,
    Extended or contracted all proportions
    To a most hideous object. Thence it came

That she whom all men praised, and whom myself,
Since I have lost, have loved, was in my eye
The dust that did offend it.

KING   Well excused.
That you did love her, strikes some scores away
From the great account; but love that comes too late,
Like a remorseful pardon slowly carried,
To the great sender turns a sour offence,
Crying 'That's good that's gone'. Our rash faults
Make trivial price of serious things we have,
Not knowing them until we know their grave.
Oft our displeasures, to ourselves unjust,
Destroy our friends and after weep their dust;
Our own love waking cries to see what's done,
While shameful hate sleeps out the afternoon.
Be this sweet Helen's knell, and now forget her.
Send forth your amorous token for fair Magdalen.
The main consents are had, and here we'll stay
To see our widower's second marriage-day.

COUNTESS
Which better than the first, O dear heaven, bless!
Or, ere they meet, in me, O nature, cease!

LAFEW
Come on, my son, in whom my house's name
Must be digested, give a favour from you
To sparkle in the spirits of my daughter,
That she may quickly come.

Bertram gives Lafew a ring

                    By my old beard
And every hair that's on it, Helen that's dead
Was a sweet creature; such a ring as this,
The last that ever I took her leave at court,
I saw upon her finger.

BERTRAM   Hers it was not.

KING
    Now pray you let me see it; for my eye,
    While I was speaking, oft was fastened to it.
    This ring was mine, and when I gave it Helen
    I bade her, if her fortunes ever stood
    Necessitied to help, that by this token
    I would relieve her. Had you that craft to rob her
    Of what should help her most?

BERTRAM   My gracious sovereign,
    However it pleases you to take it so,
    The ring was never hers.

COUNTESS   Son, on my life,
    I have seen her wear it, and she reckoned it
    At her life's rate.

LAFEW   I am sure I saw her wear it.

BERTRAM
    You are deceived, my lord, she never saw it.
    In Florence was it from a casement thrown me,
    Wrapped in a paper which contained the name
    Of her that threw it. Noble she was, and thought
    I stood engaged; but when I had subscribed
    To my own fortune, and informed her fully
    I could not answer in that course of honour
    As she had made the overture, she ceased
    In heavy satisfaction, and would never
    Receive the ring again.

KING   Plutus himself,
    That knows the touch and multiplying medicine,
    Has not in nature's mystery more science
    Than I have in this ring. 'Twas mine, 'twas Helen's,
    Whoever gave it you; then if you know
    That you are well acquainted with yourself,
    Confess 'twas hers, and by what rough enforcement
    You got it from her. She called the saints to surety
    That she would never put it from her finger
    Unless she gave it to yourself in bed,

Where you have never come, or sent it us
Upon her great disaster.

BERTRAM   She never saw it.

KING
You speak it falsely, as I love my honour,
And make conjectural fears to come into me
Which I wish to shut out. If it should prove
That you are so inhuman—it will not prove so,
And yet I know not; you did hate her deadly,
And she is dead; which nothing but to close
Her eyes myself could win me to believe,
More than to see this ring. Take him away.
My fore-past proofs, however the matter falls,
Shall tax my fears of little vanity,
Having vainly feared too little. Away with him.
We'll sift this matter further.

BERTRAM   If you shall prove
This ring was ever hers, you shall as easy
Prove that I husbanded her bed in Florence,
Where yet she never was.   *Exit, guarded*

KING
I am wrapped in dismal thinkings.

Enter a Gentleman (the Astringer)

GENTLEMAN   Gracious sovereign,
Whether I have been to blame or no, I know not:
Here's a petition from a Florentine
Who has for four or five removes come short
To tender it herself. I undertook it,
Vanquished thereto by the fair grace and speech
Of the poor suppliant who, by this, I know,
Is here attending. Her business looks in her
With an importunate visage, and she told me,
In a sweet verbal brief, it did concern
Your highness with herself.

KING   *(reading the letter)* *Upon his many protestations to*
   marry me when his wife was dead, I blush to say it, he
   won me. Now is the Count Rossillion a widower; his
   vows are forfeited to me and my honour's paid to him.
   He stole from Florence, taking no leave, and I follow
   him to his country for justice. Grant it me, O King! In
   you it best lies; otherwise a seducer flourishes, and a
   poor maid is undone.
                              Diana Capilet.

LAFEW   I will buy me a son-in-law in a fair, and toll for
   this. I'll none of him.

KING

   The heavens have thought well of you, Lafew,
   To bring forth this discovery. Seek these suitors.
   Go speedily, and bring again the Count.
                              Exeunt some attendants
   I am afraid the life of Helen, lady,
   Was foully snatched.

COUNTESS   Now justice on the doers!

                  Enter Bertram, guarded

KING

   I wonder, sir, since wives are monsters to you,
   And that you fly them as you swear them lordship,
   Yet you desire to marry.

                  Enter the Widow and Diana

                  What woman is that?

DIANA

   I am, my lord, a wretched Florentine,
   Derivèd from the ancient Capilet.
   My suit, as I do understand, you know,
   And therefore know how far I may be pitied.

WIDOW

    I am her mother, sir, whose age and honour
    Both suffer under this complaint we bring,
    And both shall cease, without your remedy.

KING

    Come hither, Count. Do you know these women?

BERTRAM

    My lord, I neither can nor will deny
    But that I know them. Do they charge me further?

DIANA

    Why do you look so strange upon your wife?

BERTRAM

    She's none of mine, my lord.

DIANA   If you shall marry
    You give away this hand, and that is mine,
    You give away heaven's vows, and those are mine,
    You give away myself, which is known mine;
    For I by vow am so embodied yours
    That she who marries you must marry me—
    Either both or none.

LAFEW   Your reputation comes too short for my daughter;
    you are no husband for her.

BERTRAM

    My lord, this is a silly, desperate creature
    Whom sometimes I have laughed with. Let your highness
    Lay a more noble thought upon my honour
    Than just to think that I would sink it here.

KING

    Sir, for my thoughts, you have them ill to friend
    Till your deeds gain them; fairer prove your honour
    Than in my thought it lies!

DIANA   Good my lord,
    Ask him upon his oath if he does think
    He had not my virginity.

KING

What say you to her?

BERTRAM   She's impudent, my lord,

And was a common gamester to the camp.

DIANA

He does me wrong, my lord; if I were so .

He might have bought me at a common price.

Do not believe him. O behold this ring

Whose high respect and rich validity

Did lack a parallel; yet for all that

He gave it to a commoner of the camp,

If I am one.

COUNTESS   He blushes and it's it.

Of six preceding ancestors, that gem

Conferred by testament to the sequent issue,

Has it been owned and worn. This is his wife:

That ring's a thousand proofs.

KING   I thought you said

You saw one here in court could witness it.

DIANA

I did, my lord, but loth am to produce

So bad an instrument: his name is Parolles.

LAFEW

I saw the man today, if man he is.

KING

Find him and bring him hither.   *Exit an attendant*

BERTRAM   What of him?

He's quoted for a most perfidious slave

With all the spots of the world taxed and debauched,

Whose nature sickens but to speak a truth.

Am I or that or this for what he'll utter,

That will speak anything?

KING   She has that ring of yours.

BERTRAM

I think she has. Certain it is I liked her

And boarded her in the wanton way of youth.

She knew her distance and did angle for me,
Madding my eagerness with her restraint,
As all impediments in fancy's course
Are motives of more fancy. And in fine
Her infinite cunning with her common grace
Subdued me to her rate. She got the ring,
And I had that which any inferior might
At market-price have bought.

DIANA   I must be patient.
You that have turned off a first so noble wife
May justly forgo me. I pray you yet—
Since you lack virtue I will lose a husband—
Send for your ring, I will return it home,
And give me mine again.

BERTRAM   I have it not.

KING

What ring was yours, I pray you?

DIANA   Sir, much like
The same upon your finger.

KING

Know you this ring? This ring was his of late.

DIANA

And this was it I gave him, being abed.

KING

The story then goes false you threw it him
Out of a casement?

DIANA   I have spoken the truth.

Enter Parolles

BERTRAM

My lord, I do confess the ring was hers.

KING

You startle swiftly; every feather starts you.—
Is this the man you speak of?

DIANA   Ay, my lord.

KING

    Tell me, fellow—but tell me true I charge you,

    Not fearing the displeasure of your master,

    Which on your just proceeding I'll keep off—

    Of him and of this woman here what know you?

PAROLLES   So please your majesty, my master has been an honourable gentleman. Tricks he has had in him, which gentlemen have.

KING   Come, come, to the purpose. Did he love this woman?

PAROLLES   Faith, sir, he did love her; but how?

KING   How, I pray you?

PAROLLES   He did love her, sir, as a gentleman loves a woman.

KING   How is that?

PAROLLES   He loved her, sir, and loved her not.

KING   As you are a knave and no knave. What an equivocal companion is this!

PAROLLES   I am a poor man, and at your majesty's command.

LAFEW   He's a good drum, my lord, but a bad orator.

DIANA   Do you know he promised me marriage?

PAROLLES   Faith, I know more than I'll speak.

KING   But will you not speak all you know?

PAROLLES   Yes, so please your majesty. I did go between them as I said; but more than that, he loved her, for indeed he was mad for her and talked of Satan and of Limbo and of furies and I know not what. Yet I was in that credit with them at that time that I knew of their going to bed and of other motions, as promising her marriage and things which would derive me ill will to speak of; therefore I will not speak what I know.

KING   You have spoken all already, unless you can say they are married. But you are too slim in your evidence— therefore, stand aside.

    This ring you say was yours?

DIANA   Ay, my good lord.
KING

  Where did you buy it? Or who gave it you?

DIANA

  It was not given me, and I did not buy it.

KING

  Who lent it you?

DIANA   It was not lent me either.

KING

  Where did you find it then?

DIANA   I found it not.

KING

  If it were yours by none of all these ways
  How could you give it him?

DIANA   I never gave it him.

LAFEW   This woman's an easy glove, my lord; she goes off
  and on at pleasure.

KING

  This ring was mine; I gave it his first wife.

DIANA

  It might be yours or hers for aught I know.

KING

  Take her away, I do not like her now.
  To prison with her. And away with him.
  Unless you tell me where you had this ring
  You die within this hour.

DIANA   I'll never tell you.

KING

  Take her away.

DIANA   I'll put in bail, my lord.

KING

  I think you now some common customer.

DIANA

  By Jove, if ever I knew man it was you.

KING
  Wherefore have you accused him all this while?
DIANA
  Because he's guilty and he is not guilty.
  He knows I am no maid, he'll swear to it;
  I'll swear I am a maid and he knows not.
  Great king, I am no strumpet; by my life
  I am either maid or else this old man's wife.
KING
  She does abuse our ears. To prison with her.
DIANA
  Good mother, fetch my bail. Stay, royal sir;
                                    Exit the Widow
  The jeweller that owns the ring is sent for
  And he shall surety me. But for this lord
  Who has abused me as he knows himself,
  Though yet he never harmed me, here I quit him.
  He knows himself my bed he has defiled,
  And at that time he got his wife with child.
  Dead though she be she feels her young one kick.
  So there's my riddle: one that's dead is quick.
  And now behold the meaning.

            Enter the Widow, with Helena

KING   Is there no exorcist
  Beguiles the truer office of my eyes?
  Is it real that I see?
HELENA   No, my good lord,
  It is but the shadow of a wife you see,
  The name and not the thing.
BERTRAM   Both, both. O pardon!
HELENA
  O my good lord, when I was like this maid
  I found you wondrous kind. There is your ring,
  And, look you, here's your letter. This it says:

When from my finger you can get this ring . . .
And is by me with child, etc. This is done.
Will you be mine now you are doubly won?

BERTRAM

If she, my liege, can make me know this clearly
I'll love her dearly, ever, ever dearly.

HELENA

If it appears not plain and prove untrue
Deadly divorce step between me and you!
O my dear mother, do I see you living?

LAFEW

My eyes smell onions, I shall weep anon.
(*To Parolles*) Good Tom Drum, lend me a handkerchief.
So, I thank you. Wait on me home, I'll make sport with
    you. Let your curtsies alone, they are scurvy ones.

KING

Let us from point to point this story know
To make the even truth in pleasure flow.
(*To Diana*) If you are yet a fresh uncroppèd flower
Choose you your husband and I'll pay your dower;
For I can guess that by your honest aid
You kept a wife herself, yourself a maid.
Of that and all the progress more and less
Resolvèdly more leisure shall express.
All yet seems well, and if it ends so meet,
The bitter past, more welcome is the sweet.

Flourish

EPILOGUE

Spoken by the King

The King's a beggar, now the play is done.
All is well ended if this suit is won,
That you express content; which we will pay
With strife to please you, day exceeding day.
Ours be your patience then and yours our parts;
Your gentle hands lend us and take our hearts.   *Exeunt*